Extraordinary Gifts, Unique Challenges

Williams Syndrome

Edited by Michelle Self, Ph.D., Vanessa Coggshall,
and Tess Roach

Published in the United States of America

ISBN-13: 978-1499101089

ISBN-10: 1499101082

1.Williams syndrome 2. Parents of children with disabilities. I. Self, Michelle. II. Title

Dedication

To everyone with Williams syndrome

and all those who care for them.

You inspire us.

"Being challenged in life is inevitable;
being defeated is optional."
—Roger Crawford

"It is your reaction to adversity, not the adversity itself,
that determines how your life's story will develop."
—Dieter F. Uchtdorf

Contents

Acknowledgments

The editors would like to especially thank Terry Monkaba and everyone at the Williams Syndrome Association for their help and support. We would also like to thank Christy Penka for her wonderful editing skills and willingness to volunteer.

Last but certainly not least, we truly appreciate all of our contributors—we would have nothing without your willingness to share your stories. Thank you!

Introduction

Williams syndrome is, technically, a genetic condition. It's not a *hereditary* one—we all learn to distinguish between the terms at some point—but a genetic one, a condition that arises from the genes. Parents and other caregivers of those who have it become rather adept at rattling off the possible physical effects: supravalvular aortic stenosis, tortuosity of renal arteries, hyperacusis, colic—oh my goodness, the colic!—low muscle tone, trouble sleeping, and on and on. And those things take up a fair amount of our time and attention in the early days. But then we get into a groove somehow, and we can start to focus on the person behind all the medical issues. That's when Williams syndrome becomes so much more than a genetic condition.

That's when it becomes wide smiles, indiscriminate *hello*s in the grocery store, well-timed hugs, concern for bumped knees, and daily lessons in loving unconditionally. That's when it takes on a larger-than-life meaning that amazes us on a regular basis. That's when we start to wonder just which people in this world have disabilities.

Of course, the challenges don't stop because we get into a groove. They keep coming, and figure them out we must. Sometimes it can be too much. That's fair. We're allowed to get overwhelmed and frustrated and even angry; some of us have been dealt pretty tough hands. But each hand has come with a bonus—a regular reminder that life is good, that there's something to be happy about, and that someone loves us.

And in the end, isn't that all that matters?

We hope that the stories in this book will remind you of days gone by, inspire you for days still to come, and even inform you about Williams syndrome in general. Wherever you are in your walk on this path, you will find a story that meets you there and, hopefully, some that help you look forward with anticipation. It truly is a beautiful path.

Enjoy the walk.

Part I

The Beginning

Chapter 1

The Diagnosis

The paths we take through life with Williams syndrome are wide and varied, but the one thing they all have in common is a point in time when the discovery was made. It happened when we got the test results back, the friend of a friend made a stunning statement, or the pieces of the puzzle finally snapped into place. At some point, we discovered that our lives would now include this term "Williams syndrome." This is when our brains, hearts, and souls were left scrambling, making sense of this new information. Our emotions ran the gamut: some felt devastated, some relieved, some befuddled, and some numb. Whatever our reactions, none of us will forget the day we got the diagnosis.

Different
Beth Kohler

Beth and Mark Kohler live in Monroe, Michigan. They have two children, John and Cameron, and enjoy living a very full, fast, furious, and glorious life. Their hobby seems to be driving their children everywhere, but in their spare time, Beth practices tae kwon do and Mark is an avid golfer.

It seems as though our story was different from the very beginning. Cameron was premature by six weeks—not so much that we kept a constant vigil in the Neonatal Intensive Care Unit but enough to keep

him in the special care nursery for ten days after he was born. At three pounds eleven ounces, he was bigger than all of his peers for one time in his life, a veritable beast among all those tiny fingers and toes. As soon as we brought him home, I popped open one of my baby shower gifts, *What to Expect the First Year.* But I couldn't find the chapter on how to find the world's tiniest diapers within a thirty-mile radius, the chapter on how to properly transport your baby when he's attached to an oxygen tank, or the one on how to disable the piercing alarm stemming from the heart monitor cord that got dislodged when I stepped on it while trying to put him back to bed at 3:00 a.m. Where were all the books and magazines on how to best measure your baby's food intake by cc's? In fact, what store could you go to at 3:00 a.m. when you discovered that your dog had eaten the only pacifier that would soothe him—the one given to him in the NICU six months earlier? There simply was no manual for this.

As time went on, I stopped even trying to read baby and parenting magazines. They were utterly depressing. My child was not represented in them. We are fortunate to have the world's most loving pediatrician, and he was utterly devoted to Cameron during his first year (and still is). But every time I questioned him about Cameron's painfully slow development, he would respond with a mathematical formula of adjusted age for babies who were premature. "Just wait," he said. "It takes early babies longer to catch up." So we waited and waited and waited. At one year, my sister and her family came to stay with us for a week, bringing my one-year-old nephew in tow. I knew the minute I saw him sitting next to Cameron that there was more going on here than meets the eye. So, the next time our Early Intervention Child Find coordinator called—a call we received regularly because he was premature—I said, "Sure, you can come for a home visit." We spent the next nine months in various forms of therapies. We got play therapy—toys could no longer be for fun; they had to have a purpose! We got occupational therapy—just put the damn dice in the tube, for crying out loud! We got physical therapy— bears crawl, not babies! This only led to more questions and few answers. Finally, because I pushed and pushed, our physical therapist broke down, violating every rule she was subject to, and told us that Cameron looked "syndromy." Umm, what?

After endless waiting in exam room after exam room, we finally had an answer. When he was twenty-two months old, we learned that Cameron had something called Williams syndrome. Believe it or not, we were actually relieved to finally have a reason for his developing so differently. Plus, we learned that there was an organization called the Williams Syndrome Association, and they were having a convention in just two months that was only forty minutes from our house in Dearborn, Michigan. So we signed up and met so many wonderful families and super cool kids. We learned that kids with WS smile a lot and that they're so friendly, happy, and musical! Some researchers even thought that maybe they had discovered the gene for joy. Who couldn't love them? Plus, so many kids have such serious health problems. We were lucky that, other than asthma resulting from being early, Cameron's supravalvular aortic stenosis was minor, and his hypercalcemia and nephrocalcinosis would eventually resolve themselves.

However, as Cameron started school, we started experiencing very challenging behavior. Where was this happy, smiley boy we used to know? And music? Not Cam—he just wasn't into it. Once again, there were no guidebooks. I kept reading "Welcome to Holland" by Emily Perl Kingsley to remind myself to appreciate the beautiful things about this country called Williams syndrome that we had landed in. But we so desperately wanted to connect and bond with others who were going through the same thing. Where were they? There had to be others out there! Fortunately, we attended another WS convention and sat in on a session about medication management. Would we really become one of those families who drugged their kid? Couldn't we do something else? But this wonderful doctor said something that was so enlightening that I never will forget it. She said, "If your child had a heart condition that needed medication, would you deny him?" *No*, I thought, *of course not!* She continued, "The brain is an organ just like the heart is, and behavioral challenges like ADD, ADHD, anxiety, and mood disorder are real conditions, so why would you deny your child medication that would help him?" It was all we needed to hear. We met with our pediatrician as soon as we got home, and he listened. And Cameron really seemed to feel better and be happier—for a while.

Now that he's on the verge of entering high school, we've had many years of experience learning that drug therapy doesn't always work. There is no magic pill, although for a while I thought that if I ever met the person who invented Prozac, I would kiss him or her full on the mouth. We would find a cocktail that would work for a while, and then Cam would grow or some situation would change, and so began again the trial and error of finding a new formula that would get us through to the next stage in his development. We learned that just because other families went to Disneyland, it wasn't the best place for us because it was too stimulating. We now know that vacations can be a real challenge because the change in schedule is just too hard, no matter how fun the place is that we are visiting. I no longer judge kids who throw tantrums in the grocery store or stare daggers at their parents. I now want to embrace them and say, "I understand. It will be okay." My husband and I have learned to tag team for just about everything. He takes one kid and I take the other, and we meet up later. We seem to have found our groove.

Cameron still doesn't fit any precast mold. He is his own unique self. Yes, he has Williams syndrome. But it is such a small part of who he really is. He is an eighth-grader who has been fully included in school since kindergarten. He has classmates who truly enjoy knowing him and being his friend. He is a Boy Scout. He is a welcomed member of his church youth group. He loves making homemade Play-Doh, slime, and silly putty. He's a collector of puzzles, gumballs, paper, and popcorn. He is the social conscience of our neighborhood. No matter how different, frustrating, difficult, and lonely this world of disability can be, I know that we are all better because there is a boy named Cameron in the world.

One Year Later

Heather Johanson

Heather Johanson is the proud mother of two boys, Parker and Reed. She lives in Pittsburgh and enjoys reading, writing, knitting, volunteering for the WSA, and serving as an administrator for the WS Support group on Facebook.

(I wrote the following piece one year following my son Reed's Williams syndrome diagnosis and published it on my blog. It was a source of release for me, a creative outlet, to deal with the emotions I was feeling as a newly diagnosed parent. I remember how hard those first years were, dealing with the constant crying, lack of sleep, and constant worry about what could be "wrong" with my developmentally delayed child—and it felt like it would never end. But it did. Slowly, life began to get easier. I made connections with other families, and their stories helped me cope and brought me hope. I hope that my story does the same. Reed is now three, going on thirteen, and brings so much joy to our lives. For the parent of a newly diagnosed child, it really does get easier. I promise.)

One year ago today started like any other. I woke the boys (because they only sleep in on days that we need to be somewhere), got them dressed, and dropped Parker off at school. Reed and I ran some errands. After picking Parker up, we headed home. I got them lunch just like usual.

The phone rang.

I felt a wave of nausea. I just knew that this was the call I had been waiting for.

The night before, I realized that it had been exactly four weeks and that I would hear something any day. We were told that it usually takes four to eight weeks.

I spent that night obsessively reading the same articles and blogs that I had discovered over the previous month after first hearing the words "Williams syndrome." I looked at picture after picture and saw hundreds of children that could have been Reed's long-lost siblings.

I just knew.

And I was right.

Me: Hello?

Caller: Hi. Is this Mrs. Johanson?

Me: Yes. This is Heather.

Caller: Hi, Heather. This is Juliann, Reed's genetic counselor from Children's.

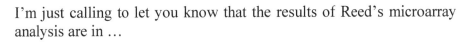

My stomach dropped.

I'm just calling to let you know that the results of Reed's microarray analysis are in …

My stomach dropped into the pit of my gut.

… and the results confirm that he does have Williams syndrome.

Whoosh. A metaphorical fist met my gut and knocked the wind out of me.

I don't remember much else about the call. I know that I asked a couple of (retrospectively) really irrelevant questions and apparently had the presence of mind to note that I needed to schedule a follow-up with his geneticist and counselor and that they wanted us to do a follow-up with cardiology as soon as possible. She must have thought I was crazy. I just couldn't manage to talk to her right then. I had been expecting the call and the result, but I guess I just wasn't ready to hear it.

After hanging up, I felt the panic attack wash over me. I couldn't breathe. I felt sick. I couldn't stop shaking. I was still trying to feed the kids and had to get them to nap. But I couldn't function.

In the two minutes that I was on the phone with Juliann, my day—and life—suddenly became like none other I had ever experienced.

I picked up the phone and called Scott. If I had to do it all over, I would wait until he got home from work. Can you imagine getting that call at work? And having to hold yourself together for the rest of the day? To this day, I still feel bad about how I handled it. I remember speaking really fast, sobbing, and then saying I couldn't talk—it was naptime, and I had to go.

I managed to get the kids napping, and I spent that time (again) obsessively reading about Williams syndrome, special needs, developmental disabilities, congenital heart defects, and anything else I could find. I found message board after message board and read about other families' experiences, but I did not reach out to anybody.

I think I waited until the next day to tell my mother, and I texted two of Reed's therapists—the ones who have been the most supportive—with the diagnosis. But it was at least a week before I told anyone else, even though I had already told friends and family that Reed was undergoing genetic testing. I just couldn't say the words.

At that time, it felt like the world that I knew was ending. Nothing would ever be the same. Reed would never have the life that all parents wish for their children.

That phase, for me, was short lived, though.

I started reaching out to family and friends, mostly through e-mail because it was so much easier to say it all in e-mail without having to answer too many questions, and I referred them to the Williams Syndrome Association website for more information. Everyone was incredibly supportive, and I started to realize that my life, my family, and my friends really weren't going to be different after all.

I started to feel more relieved than sad. I had answers. Finally.

I joined the Williams Syndrome Association and volunteered my time.

Two weeks after the call, I posted a message on a BabyCenter message board for parents of kids with chromosomal changes. I had lurked on BabyCenter for a while but never posted, so this was a big step for me. I was ready to connect with other parents and experiences. Within minutes, three mothers responded and connected me to a vast network of parents who had children with Williams syndrome on a private Facebook group. I will forever be grateful to these amazing women and mothers. I have learned so much from them, and even though we have never met in person, I feel like I've known them all my life.

The more I opened up, the more I learned and got involved, and the easier it all became. That call on February 10, 2011, really didn't change my life that much. We still had countless therapy and doctor appointments. We still had concerns about Reed's health and development. We still had concerns about Reed's future. But we also still had that sweet, amazing boy who can light up an entire room with his smile.

I realized that, yes, Reed's life will be different than what I wanted for him. But it will still be a great life filled with joy, love, and family. Different is okay. It's about him and not my wants and wishes.

Don't get me wrong. There are still (rare now, thankfully) occasions when I want to pull my hair out, cry, and scream about how unfair life is. I get burnt out with therapy and doctor appointments every now and then. I worry about Reed's health and securing a financial future for him. I stress about his upcoming IEP, advocating for him in school, fighting schools to get the services he needs, and fighting doctors' egos when determining the proper course of care. Sometimes it's all overwhelming. I don't always have my act together, but these moments have become farther and farther apart, and I spend my days now enjoying and appreciating my boys for all that they are.

One year ago, I thought my world was crumbling. But I'm still here. And I am happier, stronger, more appreciative, and more understanding than before. I am a different person now—a better person. Just one year later.

Welcome to the Family
Stacia McKeever

Stacia McKeever lives in Indiana with her husband and two sons. She enjoys gathering eggs from her chickens, finding new ways to keep the animals from her garden, tossing stones in their creek with her boys, and writing about it all.

When our son, Kieran, was diagnosed with Williams syndrome at nine months old, our family (my husband and I, as well as our extended family) went through a wide range of emotions. As we searched the Internet for information on WS, we also looked for stories that helped us know we weren't alone in what we were thinking and feeling. And we searched for hope that our baby would be okay and that his future would be bright. We were looking for something a little like this:

Dear Friend,

The news hits you like a ton of bricks, doesn't it? You feel as if you've been punched in the stomach. The air is gone, and you're trying desperately to inhale again. Somehow, you've been given a ticket to an emotional roller coaster that won't let you off, no matter how badly you want it to stop.

In a way, you're going through a grieving process. You're mourning the loss of the child you thought you had—the hopes and dreams you held for him, the unlimited potential he's had since he was born. You may even be in denial that anything is different about your child. There's probably some anger in there, as well (toward … someone? Anyone!).

And you're coming to grips with the child you now have. Suddenly, the future isn't as clear as it once was. There are no guarantees or certainties anymore. But here's the thing: Although you're not on the

14

road you initially thought you were on, we can confidently say *it's not the end of the road*. Instead, you've wandered onto a special detour from the path you were once skipping on so merrily. And we're here to tell you that this detour is filled with the beautiful scenery you would have missed had you stayed on your original path.

Sure, life will be different from what you expected even yesterday, but … (inhale deeply) *you can do this*. How do we know? We've been there. We've gotten the "genetic disorder," "developmental delays," "learning disabilities" diagnosis. The children we once viewed as perfect were also, at some point, diagnosed with Williams syndrome. Our tears were as real as the ones now pouring down *your* face. We, too, woke up in the middle of the night praying that it was all just a bad dream, wondering if somehow the doctors had read the test results wrong and we weren't really the parents of a child with special needs, a child with life-threatening physical problems.

But, as will happen with you, somehow, our pain began to subside ever so slowly. The tears began to dry up, and we began to come to grips with the diagnosis and what that meant for our families. As we did, you'll research Williams syndrome until you feel as if you could write a book on it (a good place to start is http://www.williams-syndrome.org). And you'll remember that the child now slapped with a "label" is still the child you've loved from the beginning.

Walking, talking, self-feeding, becoming potty trained, riding a bike, sleeping through the night, making friends, playing instruments (drums, harmonica, piano—you name it!), enjoying school, finding meaningful employment, attending college (check out Berkshire Hills Music Academy)—these are things that people with Williams syndrome have accomplished. Who knows what your child may accomplish!

You'll want to get your child as much help now as possible. This could involve enrolling her in occupational therapy, speech therapy, and physical therapy (check with your local Early Intervention or First Steps programs for help), as well as finding doctors in your area who are familiar with Williams syndrome and can help treat or monitor your child's symptoms. And you'll want to get help for yourself in the form of support: you can visit the WS community on Facebook.

Although it's tempting to want to know *now* to what extent your child will be affected by WS (especially if you received the diagnosis early in his life), and although we'd love to tell you based on our experiences to what extent your child will be affected, we simply can't. Just as each typically developing child is unique and develops according to his own schedule, your child is also one of a kind and will travel his own path with your help and encouragement. We've learned to take each day as it comes and to do the best that we can in this moment.

Although you may feel as if you're the only one going through this, we're here to tell you that you're not alone. We've been there and still are there, walking together and offering encouragement and help when we can. The journey is different for everyone, but it's a journey we'd be delighted to share with you and your loved ones.

Welcome to the family!

Unexpected Features
Vanessa Coggshall

Vanessa Coggshall lives in New Jersey with her husband, Dan, and two daughters, Charlotte and Emmy. She loves writing her blog, Williams Syndrome Smile (www.williamssyndromesmile.com), and aspires to complete a memoir about embracing her daughter's special needs.

Shortly after Emmy was born, I could tell that something was different about our little girl. One of my earliest indications came when she was in the NICU because her lungs hadn't transitioned smoothly to the outside world. Our nurse joked that she'd never seen a temper like Emmy's. Though she was only five pounds, Emmy turned red in the face and shrieked at the top of her lungs every time our well-meaning nurse tried to change her diaper.

But on this day, when my parents came to visit, Emmy was content to lie in my dad's arms, offering the nurse a brief reprieve from the screaming fits she'd been throwing since she'd been taken out of my cozy womb. In Grandpa's comfortable arms, Emmy's eyes were contentedly closed, and she appeared to be sleeping. Quite unexpectedly, a wide grin spread across her face. My heart stopped. This grin was larger than any other smile I'd seen. Further, it was so unlike my smile or my husband's smile. It was as if she knew a deep secret and was keeping it to herself.

My dad's eyes met mine, and I could see that we were both alarmed at her wide grin. Of course, everyone loves to see a baby's smile, but this

felt unnerving. It was different, and I was afraid of different. A few hours later, I was holding Emmy and noticed that her pinky fingers turned in. I asked the doctors about it, but no one was concerned. I surmised that I was just being a paranoid parent.

After eight long days, the doctors discharged Emmy from the NICU and told me that there was absolutely nothing amiss with my daughter.

They concluded that she was perfectly healthy and would have no limitations in life. As a side note, they mentioned that she had a slight heart murmur, which would likely dissipate on its own. However, they told us to follow up with a cardiologist in one month—part of the usual protocol. I let out a sigh of relief as I snuggled close to my daughter. We were finally taking her home.

For the next month, we endured the piercing screams of little Emmy. Nothing could soothe our unhappy baby. There was not even a trace of that sudden wide grin from the NICU. Now, she just shrieked day and night. I thought back to the nurse's prescient words—she had *never seen a temper like Emmy's*. Well, I thought, at least this feistiness will serve her well in life!

One late night, I was sitting with Emmy in our rocking chair until she finally fell asleep. I stared at her in the darkness and searched her face for some resemblance to my own. I didn't find any. A nagging feeling came knocking. Why didn't my daughter look as much like me as I thought she would?

When my husband, Dan, and I took her for the requisite first visit with her pediatrician, the doctor looked her over from head to toe, turning her little body around in his strong hands. Finally, he proclaimed, "She appears to be very healthy, except for this heart murmur." He paused and then added, "I also noticed that she has small eyes."

The doctor ushered us out and, feeling bruised and insulted, we retreated to the car. Everyone knows that when you see a baby, the appropriate comment is, "Oh, how beautiful!" Why would he say that her eyes were "small" without a positive adjective alongside? I would've even accepted "delicate," which has a much nicer ring to it. I couldn't figure out his motives but, as soon as we got home, I started searching for a new pediatrician.

At the end of the month, we dutifully attended Emmy's scheduled cardiologist appointment. I'd already researched the details of her heart murmur and discovered that it's very common for babies to have benign murmurs that disappear after a few months. I had finally stopped worrying and starting accepting the fact that she was undeniably healthy, as everyone had told me.

That cardiologist appointment changed everything.

We found out that in addition to the murmur, Emmy had narrowing in her arteries, something that had gone undetected before. Moreover, the cardiologist told us that Emmy might have a genetic disorder called Williams syndrome. But she cautioned us from jumping to conclusions until we could get an official blood test.

Dan and I drove home in disbelief and confusion. When we got back to the house, I sat on the couch with Emmy in my arms and searched for "Williams syndrome" online. I found images that depicted the facial features that accompany this diagnosis. I pored over the pictures and compared them to my little girl. I found a list of traits that are common in Williams syndrome, and when I reached the bullet point that read "wide smile," I froze. Could it be?

I still wasn't convinced. But then I read about the pinky fingers that can turn in, and that gave me further pause. And finally, I came upon one feature I had never noticed—a stellate pattern in the eyes. Surely, Emmy didn't have a pattern in her eyes. I would have detected it. As if in slow motion, I looked from the image on the screen to the baby resting in my arms.

"Emmy," I said softly, waiting for her to glance up.

She opened her eyes and looked straight at me. I felt my pulse quicken as I stared into a perfect stellate pattern. I didn't have to wait for the blood test to know why my baby didn't look like me. In an instant, I stepped through the door of a new journey, clutching on to what I used to believe and frightened of what I didn't know.

As time passed, I learned about Williams syndrome and how wonderful it really is. I made friends in this tight-knit community and got essential advice from others who have walked this path before. Early on, a parent told me that I would eventually be grateful for the diagnosis. At the time, I couldn't understand how that would be possible. But now, I know that parent was right.

Today, Emmy is almost a year and a half old, and she is a beautiful, spunky, funny, loving girl. When we go to the grocery store, everyone stops to comment on how cute she is. People will gaze at her shining, bright blue eyes and gush, "Look at those pretty eyes!" People also notice her full lips and say, "And those gorgeous lips!" Neither of these are my features. They are both gifts of Williams syndrome.

And then there's that wide grin that startled me in the beginning. Now, it melts my heart. It's true that she doesn't look just like me, but I can't imagine her looking any other way. Emmy is who she is, not who I am, though I'm told she'll develop much more of a family resemblance as she grows older. Everyone already says that she looks just like my husband.

Recently, I was feeding her at the kitchen table. I smiled at my sweet daughter and wondered how, a little over a year ago, I could have been so devastated by this diagnosis. As if on cue, Emmy caught my glance and spread her lips into her famous big grin, showing off a few white teeth. Then she reached her arms out and pulled me in for a tight hug.

She Is Perfect to Me
Colleen Riley

Colleen Riley has two daughters, Alexis (who has Williams syndrome, born in April 2009) and Alivia (born in September 2012). She is stationed near Boston, and loves to craft, shop, and coffee.

I was induced at forty-two weeks with Alexis; she was not coming out on her own! She was perfect to me. The doctors checked her over and said they wanted to do further testing on her because she had a couple of birthmarks, an extra rib, and a heart murmur, and she also hadn't passed her hearing test. They found that she had hypothyroidism and would need to have a follow-up with the cardiology and audiology departments. They said this was all common and nothing to worry about.

She got an okay from cardiology and follow-ups with audiology. I thought, *I can deal with this—a couple of blood tests and a pill every day. We can do this!*

Several months passed, and we mostly just dealt with audiology. She was put under general anesthesia for hearing tests (ABR) and had tubes put in her ears. We also discovered that she was developmentally delayed, so we started early intervention services. She was still perfect to me!

When Lexi, as we called her, was seventeen months old, her pediatrician decided that she should see multiple specialists, including an American cardiologist (we were stationed overseas with the military at the time), because her heart murmur was getting louder. They sent us to Hawaii to see a cardiologist, endocrinologist, audiologist, geneticist, and developmental pediatrician. We were also scheduled for an MRI.

They found that she had SVAS. I could tell something was wrong by the technician's face. She was scanning Lexi and then looked serious and said she was going to get the cardiologist. The cardiologist told me that she would need open-heart surgery and soon. He also said that he suspected she had Williams syndrome. I went back to my hotel room and researched Williams syndrome, like everyone does. I instantly knew: this is my little girl.

Alexis's surgery took place two weeks later. She was in the hospital for seven days, and everything went great. She has overcome multiple obstacles since then—some big, some small, but she always overcomes. She has been in preschool for about a year now and has exploded. She is now speaking in short sentences, singing songs, running, and jumping. She is my superstar. Everyone who meets her simply falls in love with her. I was honestly devastated in the beginning simply because I didn't know what it would be like for Alexis, but I have come to realize that she is a true blessing. She is still perfect to me and always will be!

It Is What It Is
Tami Hartman

Tami Hartman has two children, Esteban, who is fifteen, and Emma, who is two. She lives in Dallas, Texas. She loves watching movies and spending time with her friends and family.

On August 17, 2011, our daughter was born. The first thing that caught our attention was her bright, red, full lips. We thought, *Where did those come from?* As they moved her to the warming table, we could see that the doctors and nurses were concerned. Within a few minutes, one of the nurses came to us and told us that the baby had a cyst under her tongue and that she would go straight to the NICU. Within four hours, we were transferred to a children's hospital to receive more specific care. Seven hours later, we were informed that she had a duplicate cyst that was blocking her airways. It was heartbreaking to hear that she would need to have surgery as soon as she was stable. She was five pounds, twelve ounces at the time. Later that day, a geneticist examined our baby girl. She mentioned that she had some unusual features and that she had a very loud heart murmur. She suggested that we consider genetic testing. Overwhelmed by emotions, we agreed to the tests. We felt like we were at the mercy of anyone who looked at or cared for our baby girl. As of this time, that was her name, Baby Girl. We could not decide between Emma and Gabriela.

The doctors asked repeatedly for a name. We explained that we were waiting to see her personality because if she was going to be laid back and sophisticated, she was going to be Emma, but if she was going to be a talker and a handful, we were going with Gabriela. The doctor said, "What you see is what you get. This is her with no medication."

The next day, our baby girl was about to have the cyst removed. We felt it was necessary to name her before the surgery. We named her Emma.

About a week later, we received a phone call at home and were informed that Emma has Williams syndrome. Of course, that night we did a lot of research, and our hearts broke. All of the dreams we had for her became uncertain. She was not going to be a doctor. She was not going to be a teacher. She was not going to experience college, parties, boyfriends, or childbirth or have a wedding. Some of the information on the Internet implied that she would live with us forever and would be severely delayed.

That weekend, we asked our immediate family to come to our house for a family meeting. It was a day that no one will ever forget. Emma's uncle was holding her when we informed them that Emma was going to be a little different, but we would love her just the same. We explained that she may be a little slower, but we will never let her know that she is less than perfect. She may have different facial characteristics and be a little smaller, but we will never treat her differently. That day, tears filled everyone's eyes, and hugs were exchanged all around the room as we mourned the loss of so much. I remember every family member wanting to hold her. Whether they were saying a secret prayer or something else, everyone wanted to have his or her personal time with Emma.

The most eye-opening experience we have to share with other parents whose child may have been diagnosed with William syndrome occurred when we went in for a follow-up appointment with the doctor who had removed Emma's cyst. He asked how she was doing. We explained that she was diagnosed with Williams syndrome. His response was, "Hmm. Well … it is what it is." That was that! He said no more. Five simple words: "It is what it is!" We looked at him and thought, "Yep … it is what it is." From that day on, we accepted the challenges of having a child with Williams syndrome and agreed to relax, stop stressing, and enjoy her every day because she is our greatest gift. Life got a lot easier from the moment we accepted that we could not compare her to anyone else and stopped doing so. She *was* going to have challenges. She *was* going to be smaller and slower, but according to research, she *was* going to be one of the most loving people we would ever meet.

24

At four months old, Emma had open-heart surgery for supravalvular aortic stenosis, and since then she has had three heart catheterizations. At nine months old, she had her tear ducts probed, and at one year old she had tubes placed in her tear ducts. Even though Emma's life has been full of medical procedures, nothing—and I mean *nothing*—can wipe the big smile from her face. You know the big smile I am talking about. You've seen it. Everybody who sees Emma's smile comments on how beautiful her smile is or how much it brightens up a room. We say to ourselves, *If they only knew it was a "Williams" smile, they would see that her greatest gift will be her biggest challenge.*

Overall, I think Emma is loved more since her diagnosis; she is not just another grandchild, niece, cousin, or friend's daughter. She is the one that everyone will push to prove that, although she has Williams syndrome, she is destined for greatness.

Oh, by the way, Emma is not so much an "Emma." She is 100 percent a "Gabby." She is all over the place. She controls our house. She yells, plays, smiles, and does everything any other child does. She just happens to have Williams syndrome.

"Welcome to Holland"
Kristina Malton

Kristina lives in Oregon. She is a mom to three wonderful boys and counting.

Alexander was hospitalized with meningitis at five weeks old. While we were there, his doctor asked my permission to run some tests. They did a new hearing test, some heart tests, and some blood work. We went home when he was six weeks old, and the next week we went in for a follow-up appointment. The doctor said, "I want to talk to you about Williams syndrome." She explained that Alex had several common characteristics of Williams but said, "Let's not jump to conclusions."

Of course, I went straight home and started to read anything and everything I could find on Williams syndrome. I really didn't see what she was talking about, although Alex did have a wide smile and starburst eyes. I got the call confirming Alex had WS when he  was eight weeks old, and I burst into tears and couldn't speak. I hung up on the doctor, sank to the floor, and cried. A million questions and feelings ran through me. *They're wrong!* I thought. *How could this happen? I took care of myself when I was pregnant. What did I do wrong? Is he going to die? What kind of life will he have? How is this going to change my other children's lives? How will I afford all this? How are other people going to treat him?* There were many more thoughts as well.

The next few weeks were a blur of no sleep and learning everything I could about WS. I didn't tell anyone. A friend came up to me after a softball game and very boldly said, "Okay, what's going on? Is something wrong with Alex?" I lost it and told him everything that had happened. He said, "Welcome to Holland." I had no idea what he was talking about. He told me about the essay by Emily Perl Kingsley and that he had a little sister with Down syndrome. He told me how wonderful this would be when I got past the shock. He also said how incredible it was to be the brother of a child with special needs. He said that the dreams I had for Alex before knowing about WS weren't gone—they just needed to be changed a little.

I went home and found the "Welcome to Holland" essay online. At that moment, I got over the diagnosis and changed my way of thinking. I put Alex into physical therapy right away. The therapist would tell me to expect him to accomplish certain tasks around certain ages, but Alex always learned them earlier. He's almost three now and is the happiest little boy I've ever known. He has to say "hi" to every person we pass. His smile lights up the room. I can be in an "off" mood, and he'll come over and hug me. Somehow, Williams syndrome enables our kids to approach the world with a happy-go-lucky attitude. I wish everyone had a WS personality. Williams syndrome is truly a gift, and I wouldn't change it if I could.

Our Village

Tracy Mason

Tracy Mason and her husband, Brad, live in Fairfax, Virginia, with their two children, Katherine and Jonathan. She enjoys reading for work and fun, regular "Mason family dance parties," and traveling with her family. You can follow her on Facebook or Twitter @traymay5.

Catch Your Breath

"It takes a village to raise a child." Whether it's an old African proverb or the title of a popular book, I have found that this phrase describes how life has presented itself to my family. As you read about our "village," I hope it provides comfort that, as you catch your breath, anything is possible when you have built a strong village.

I'll never forget the first time I heard the words "Williams syndrome." Some of you heard them within days of your child's birth. In our case, it was almost a year into Jon's life when his eye doctor suggested we look into a myriad of symptoms to identify a connection.

As the geneticist said those words to my husband and me, I caught my breath. That day, we opened a door to what, at the time, was a great unknown. I looked down at my little baby boy—so many questions to be answered. And that is when Jon's village started to be built.

Brick by Brick

At first, I absorbed the facts: this condition is random, rare. What impact will these missing genes have on Jon's life? We wondered, *How will Jon respond and rise to the challenges that come his way?*

Then we learned, thanks to many talented medical and academic professionals who specifically study Williams syndrome, what to look for, ask about, and do to address each bend in the road. It's a road map of sorts that helped build the foundation for the village. For

28

someone who likes to have a plan, it meant a lot of work, meetings, and questions. I took a deep breath … and dove right in.

It was quite overwhelming at first. And then, something wonderful happened. We met people who offered to help us "build."

We were lucky. Early on, we talked to another "builder"—a parent whose child also had WS and who was willing to share his blueprints, opening a window for us to others who lived in this village. (Thanks, Alex.)

Then, we met very good doctors—more than we ever expected to know—who drew heart diagram after diagram to show where the narrowing occurred or what the eye surgery would entail. They patiently answered the endless rounds of questions. We also encountered therapists who taught us a new language to help Jon learn to walk and talk, hold a crayon, even fasten buttons. And although the load was heavy, we caught our breath, adding brick by brick to our village.

Celebrating Milestones in the Village

Our definition of *milestone* changed, expanded. I joyfully remember not just Jon's first steps but also his first steps without shoe inserts or foot braces. And I remember not just sleeping through the night but also when Jon first slept through the night in his own bed for a week straight. You get the picture. And our whole village celebrated these milestones with us.

Like it says in the "Welcome to Holland" essay by Emily Perl Kingsley, once someone you love receives a diagnosis that affects his growth and development, you're brought into a place you might not have been aware of before. Up to that point, we'd been living our lives, oblivious to this expanded world within both the medical and educational communities. However, once you do meet people who help you learn your way, the drive for advocacy to expand others' understanding takes hold, and your village begins to clear a path to foster awareness.

As you tell people you know about Williams syndrome, your village grows. I am so very thankful to have such supportive family, friends, and neighbors who have embraced learning about and graciously supporting our efforts to understand and share the joys and challenges of Williams syndrome as they present themselves in our lives. Whether it was coworkers who staffed a WSA fund-raising gala, a church who developed a special needs ministry program, or a daycare center that spread WS awareness with wrapping paper fund-raisers— each did its part for our village. And it makes my heart swell.

Candidly, I feel blessed by the true joy and love that Jon presents to this village in his strong hugs, wide and sincere smiles, and abundant excitement for what is most important to him. For as much as he continues to evolve and grow, all in our village have learned much about themselves and what is truly important from him.

Emotion and Inspiration in the Village

Thanks to technology, the village has expanded globally with information provided, at times, within moments of asking. I am so very thankful for those who've paved the way—WSA moms like Terry, Debbie, Nanci, and Michelle who tirelessly share their parenting experiences and their children's journeys to inspire and support other WS families across the country and around the world. Knowing that "back then" there was limited Internet research and idea-sharing support groups to both learn from and post to makes the villages they've built even more wonderful to visit.

I can't remember which WSA national convention presentation I was in when I heard this, or whether I asked the question or another parent offered it up. Either way, it was a game-changer for both Jon and me: "How does a person with WS cope through the range of intense emotions?" Its answer helped me recognize what building block I would use to construct our village. "Keep telling them to catch their breath," the presenter said. "This phrase will help them focus and calm them down." This self-calming mechanism works like magic with Jon who, as you might imagine, can get pretty emotional at times. And it helps me work through my feelings too.

Ironically, Jon never really got into building things. Other than for the developmental tests, he has never taken to playing with traditional blocks. And when we built block towers together, he couldn't wait to laugh and knock them down just as the tower was at its tallest. I may be building the village, but it's Jon who is the glue to hold it together. With each accomplishment, he still takes my breath away! I have to keep reminding myself, *Catch your breath.* But after living in this village for a while now, I've learned to add another part to the phrase—*Catch your breath, and enjoy the ride.*

Chapter 2

Surgeries, Medical Issues, and Early Intervention

So much of the focus on Williams syndrome, perhaps justifiably, is on what many have called the "joy gene"—on how those with Williams syndrome feel happiness to a greater extent than others and are so adept at spreading that joy to others. However, often hidden beneath that happiness is a heart that's been through surgery, as well as numerous other health issues that have been encountered along the way. Thankfully, modern medicine is significantly helping correct Williams syndrome–related problems and improving quality of life, with effects on those with Williams syndrome that are remarkable.

Healing Hearts
Amanda Fuller

Amanda Fuller lives in Ohio with her husband and two children. She enjoys spending lots of time with her family and friends.

How do you describe the love of your life? Try it. It's almost impossible to put into words a worthy description that does him or her any bit of justice. The love of my life is a blond-haired, blue-eyed, three-foot-tall little man named Wyatt. Since the moment he came into our lives on a sunny June day in 2009, my husband and I have been enamored by him and enlightened merely by his presence.

Wyatt was diagnosed with Williams syndrome in February of 2010. Of course, no one around us had heard of such a thing. There were moments of disappointment in the beginning—my husband would probably not have a star quarterback playing for the Ohio State Buckeyes or the genius who would finally find the cure for cancer. We needed to find out what kind of person we would have, so we did the

best thing we could do and armed ourselves with all the information we could find. What we found was eye-opening, to say the least. Our son would be musical, animated, fun-loving, friendly, empathetic, and most important, kind to others. Our disappointments quickly diminished, and what replaced them was prideful anticipation for what a lovely human being our child would become.

On July 29, 2010, when Wyatt was just thirteen months old, he underwent open-heart surgery to repair his supravalvular aortic stenosis. Our whole family was with us that day as we said silent prayers that the child who had stolen our hearts would have his own repaired and come out as healthy as ever. We were given hourly updates, one of which contained the scariest words a parent could ever hear: "He is on bypass now. His heart is not pumping." My son's heart was not pumping, and at that moment, I thought mine would stop too.

What seemed like an eternity later—but in actuality was about four hours—another update arrived. "He is off of bypass, and his heart started pumping again!" His. Heart. Started. Pumping. Again. The five most beautiful words I had ever heard in my entire life! After nearly eight hours away from our son, we were finally able to see him. We walked into the PICU room, and there he was, sweetly nestled in a hospital bed and hooked up to monitors and a ventilator, a sight no parent should ever see. His swollen little body was recovering from a trauma that was so impossible to wrap our minds around. His tiny heart was on the mend; all the while ours were breaking at the sight of him. The few, seemingly endless days following the surgery were filled with anxiety, tears, fear, and realizations that our son would never truly be like all the other kids.

Very slowly, glimmers of our energetic little boy started to appear, and the prayers became exclamations of our undying gratefulness. After only four days in the hospital, we were released to go home and resume life as usual. Wyatt was back to his normal, endearing self after about a week, and you would never know he had been through such a trial. While I would never want to relive those days of agony, I am very grateful to have experienced that time. What a miraculous experience! Our son's life was saved by the hands of two human beings. I have never in all my life felt closer to God.

The common assumption when parents receive a diagnosis pointing toward special needs is that they would be devastated. I'll admit that I, too, used to assume that is how I would feel. What I have found since Wyatt's WS diagnosis, however, is that there are a few things that help you navigate this new, albeit slightly scary, crazy life on which you're about to embark: patience, knowledge, family, prayer, and *optimism*!

My son will be turning five soon, and in these last five years, my heart has swelled, broken, and been healed a hundred times over—all because of that little blond-haired, bouncing baby boy. He has made our lives and the lives of everyone who has been lucky enough to cross his path so much richer. He has taught us in such a short amount of time so much more than we will ever be able to teach him. He has made every day a sunny day. He has filled our hearts with so much

34

joy, and we count ourselves lucky to have him. There is not a single day that goes by that I don't thank God for making Wyatt, for entrusting us with this special boy, and most of all for choosing me to be his mommy.

Heartscape
Jill Calian

Jill Calian lives in Illinois with her husband, Phil, and four sons, Luke, Sam, Christian and Julian. Jill is a special education lawyer.

My husband and I are standing in a darkened laboratory at Chicago Children's Memorial Hospital staring at the grainy screen that reveals the state of our son's heart. Our two-year-old, Julian, is having an echocardiogram. The purpose of this test is to tell us whether his pulmonary stenosis, a narrowing of the artery leading from the right ventricle to the lungs, has progressed to the point where he will require open-heart surgery.

We are peering over the shoulder of the lab technician at a gray screen that depicts a cross-section of Julian's heart. Or at least, that's what I think it is showing. All I really know is that the lab technician is gliding a jellied probe across the small chest of my son, and blurry

images of a pulsating orb are showing up on the screen. It resembles an aerial view of two boxers rhythmically jabbing at each other.

On the bottom of the screen, there is a bright green line that looks like something Julian would draw on his Etch-a-Sketch. But the line is moving, repeating a wave pattern over and over again. I assume this is his heartbeat, and I am reassured by its beautiful regularity.

Bright colors—red, orange, and green—are flaring up on the screen. They look like the Doppler weather maps on the nightly news. Is that a tropical storm moving across Julian's heart?

Trying to lighten things up, my husband makes a joke about "Saturday night at the movies." He's right; this is like twenty minutes at a foreign film with no subtitles. That gives me an idea: maybe I'm better at reading faces than screens. I give up squinting at the screen and start scrutinizing the technician for clues about what she perceives. She doesn't show any; her face remains placidly professional. Of course, I could inquire, "How does it look?" But she would beg off, tell us that the cardiologist will explain the results to us later. Knowing this would only make our anxiety worse, I say nothing. We wait.

I wonder what a scan of my own heart would look like at this moment. I'm sure it would reveal a quickened rhythm, betraying my anxiety. But would it show how much I love this little boy? Would this film of my heart capture the throbbing, breaking way it feels right now?

I turn to look at Julian. Miraculously, he's sleeping through this whole procedure. Earlier today, before this test began, I climbed up on the exam table in this dim, overheated room, held him close to me, and sang him his favorite lullaby over and over again. "Hush little baby, don't say a word …" Don't worry because Mommy can fix everything. How I wish that were true.

The lullaby did its magic, and Julian finally dropped off to sleep. He's sleeping blissfully now, lying on his back, his arms above his head in the "surrender" position. His breathing is steady and calm. Surely he is too peaceful, too beautiful for anything to be wrong.

I remember that a couple of years ago, I was the one on the exam table, the cold ultrasound probe moving across my belly. I was pregnant with Julian and his twin brother, Christian. Then, as now, I stared at the ultrasound pictures trying to make some sense out of them. Julian (known then as "Baby B") was inexplicably smaller than his twin. The obstetrician was concerned, and so were we.

But, other than the disparate size of the babies, the pregnancy was healthy. I delivered the twins when they were 37-1/2 weeks, almost term for a twin pregnancy. Except for a slight heart murmur, Julian seemed fine, as did Christian. Three days later we brought home two healthy, albeit tiny, baby boys to join their two older brothers.

But Julian didn't grow as fast as his twin brother. And he didn't develop as quickly either. Christian always seemed to be a couple of developmental steps ahead of him. Julian had a few other health issues. He was briefly very ill with a respiratory virus. He developed an inguinal hernia that was surgically repaired. And his heart murmur worsened, leading to a diagnosis of moderate supravalvular pulmonary stenosis. When Julian was nine months old, his pediatrician suggested that we consult with a geneticist. When I probed, the doctor told me that he suspected that Julian might have a genetic disorder called Williams syndrome.

Of course I went directly home and Googled "Williams syndrome." I saw the faces of the children on the WSA website. They looked more like Julian's "twin" than his actual twin brother. Before I even read the text on the website, I knew. I knew at that moment, long before we received the positive FISH test results from the geneticist, that Julian had Williams syndrome.

But knowing is not the same as understanding. Knowing happens in a flash. Acceptance takes longer. It's harder. It requires tears and grief, but eventually, inevitably, it dawns.

Julian will have a challenging life. But for now, he is a radiant child— a guileless boy who runs and jumps, giggles, squeals with joy, romps with his three brothers, and charms strangers with his smile. I know that he has a "genetic disorder," that he is "cognitively impaired," and that he has a "heart defect," but I refuse to see this boy as fundamentally flawed. It's not that I think he doesn't have faults—he has many; it's that I've come to realize that he is simply and exactly who he is meant to be. There is a place in this world for Julian just as he is, and in some ways—that will continue to unfold as he lives his life—we are better because of him.

The echocardiogram is over, and the cardiologist is coming into the lab to discuss the results with us. The doctor tells us that Julian's stenosis has not gotten any worse. There is no need for surgery as long as the pulmonary artery does not constrict any further. We don't have to come back for another echo for six months.

Be still, my beating heart.

Kaleidoscope
Colleen Kilcullen

Colleen Kilcullen and her husband, Rock Fritz, live in Longmont, Colorado, with their three sons, Keller, Becket, and Bridger. She has been a nurse for over ten years and is currently finishing her master's degree in nursing.

"A kaleidoscope of emotions" was the phrase used by a fellow mother of a child with Williams syndrome to describe the first year of her son's life. A kaleidoscope is characterized by forms that are in constant flux, transforming shards of darkness and light, and strange yet beautiful patterns—certainly an accurate description of the journey

we have shared with our beautiful son, Bridger. As we prepare for the birth of our children, we overflow with emotions—excitement, anticipation, joy. When it becomes clear that our most basic desire and expectation for our children, the declaration of good health, is unfulfilled, there is a spiral of grief and devastation. I suffered a great deal of heartache in the first months of Bridger's life, but it quickly became apparent that I needed to let go of my expectations and preconceptions and celebrate my child. His cardiologist suspected Williams syndrome when he was just five days old. Genetic testing would later confirm the diagnosis, though the images we found of children with Williams, with their sweet elfin faces, were identical to Bridger. We had no question that this was what we were dealing with, and we began our journey toward acceptance.

At three months of age, Bridger was hospitalized for a life-threatening respiratory virus. He spent his first Christmas in the hospital, and, admittedly, it was difficult to suppress the sadness I felt for my son and for my family. Six weeks later, he underwent a complex open-heart surgery. Witnessing his recovery, it was impossible not to recognize his resilience and fortitude. We watched and waited through several agonizing days as his heart mended, and soon his wide smile and bright eyes reappeared. When we brought him home a week after his surgery and I was blessed with the realization that Bridger would have no problem overcoming the challenges he may face in life, there was a fog that lifted from my heart. Our kaleidoscope of emotions, which seemed to have been filled with particularly dark, distorted shards, gave way to brightness and light—more gentle transformations. Despite the overwhelming exhaustion and anxiety, we emerged from those early months with an indescribable joy in the spirit and strength of our son. We gained a perspective that can only be understood among parents of children with serious illness and disability. The typical concerns of parenthood, desires to raise children that are intellectually gifted or athletically talented, seemed remarkably trivial and obsolete. The idea that somehow we are in control of all aspects of our children's lives—their health, their abilities, their achievements—dissolved. This awareness has proven to be truly liberating. The love we have for our children is no longer restrained by expectations or perceptions of control.

Bridger is now an energetic two-year-old who embodies the "cocktail party" social characteristics shared by our children with Williams syndrome. He finds great joy in greeting others, in sharing his exuberance, and in receiving a smile. His expressions of love are so passionate and sincere; it is impossible to ignore the light that radiates from his precious soul. As a parent and as an individual, I find myself to be gentler, more empathic, and more accepting. I am living in the present more than ever, though I do occasionally allow myself to envision Bridger's future and become filled with excitement. I am certain he will achieve great things and fill many hearts with love.

Open-Heart Surgery

Sherry Grover

Sherry is mom to four young boys: Brody, Brennan, Cooper, and Carson. She lives in Toledo, Ohio, and enjoys reading, crocheting, and spending time with her "monkeys."

Brody had open-heart surgery at the ripe old age of four months. Earlier, as we sat with him while he was having a sedated echocardiogram, the surgeon walked in, looked at the screen, and said, "That looks like Williams syndrome. We'd better get a heart cath to check the pressures." So my husband and I took our sleeping (sedated) baby back to the waiting room until he could be called for the cath. Greg lay with Brody on his chest because we didn't dare move for fear that we would wake him. He hadn't been able to eat since midnight the night before, and we knew he would be miserable. When the nurse came and took him, it was well into the afternoon. Brody was gone for hours, so Greg and I had nothing to do but sit and wait by ourselves in the waiting room. While we were waiting, our family started to arrive from out of town. We all sat as patiently as possible.

Finally the doctor arrived, well past five o'clock that afternoon. Greg and I sat huddled together as the doctor delivered the news. Surgery would be the best option; he laid out the plans for what was to be done. Brody was scheduled for eight o'clock the following morning, and because it was so late in the day, he would have to spend the night to make sure he came out of the anesthesia okay after the cath. Greg decided that he would be the one to sit with him through the night. After seeing my baby and holding him tight while he finally drank a bottle, I left with my parents for a restless night at the hotel.

The next morning arrived, and I returned to the hospital with my mom in tow. I was a mess because I had no idea what was going to happen to my baby. Sure, I knew what they had told me, but the fear of the unknown had grabbed hold and was still holding on

tightly. We had a quick baptism at the side of Brody's bed to make sure that faith would help him through. Before I knew it, they were walking us down to the surgery floor, where we were directed to a little cubicle to do the final pre-op. I felt so blessed that they let me hold him all the way. Looking back, I barely remember anything about that time. I do remember an anesthesiologist coming to talk to my husband and me, but I do not remember a word that was said. I just held onto my baby, sobbing and whispering to him over and over, "Mommy loves you. Mommy needs you to be so strong. The doctors are going to take good care of you." I held him like this until it was time to take him back. My poor husband could only give him a kiss on the forehead. I wasn't letting go any earlier than I had to.

Greg and I went up to the Pediatric Cardiac Intensive Care Unit, where the waiting game began. Our family filled the whole room. We waited and waited as the hours passed by for some word that he was done and that he had been amazing. Some other parent told Greg and me to take a tour of the unit in order to prepare ourselves for what we would see after the surgery—the best advice I got. If I had not done that, I would not have been prepared. Those precious little babies were all hooked up to monitors, tubes, and machines. The child life specialist also told us all the rules of the Pediatric Cardiac Care Unit—call before you enter, wash your hands, and so on. After five *long* hours, the surgeon returned to my family. Brody had done great! She told us all the things that she had done to help our son and that she would check back on him in the next couple of days. They were bringing him up from surgery, and it would be an hour before they would let us back to see him. My mom quickly ushered me out for a walk, knowing that I was about to lose it again, this time in relief over what an amazingly strong little boy I had and what he had overcome.

My friend who was a NICU nurse at this hospital knew that a shift change was coming. Fifty-five minutes after I spoke to the doctor, my friend told me to call in to the nurses' station and request entry because they did not allow anyone to come into the unit during a shift change. If you were in, you could stay, but you could not come in afterward. So I called, and initially they told me no, but I begged and they said that they would allow us to come back for a few minutes. I walked back, and there was my precious little baby lying on a sterile hospital bed with his chest covered in bandages. No one could have prepared a mom for that sight. I touched his little hand and just cried with relief while the nurse continued to clean him up. My family took turns rotating in and out to see Brody. The thing I remember most is one of Greg's aunts crying after leaving him and saying how no baby should have to go through that.

Brody didn't have an easy recovery from this procedure. The pain medication gave him insomnia. We walked the hospital floor until three o'clock in the morning, when a wonderful nurse finally told me she would watch him for a couple of hours so I could sleep in his room on a bench. That was the end of the pain medication. We ended up back in the hospital after only two days of being home. Poor Brody just wasn't ready. We spent an additional week at a hospital closer to home. Brody never drank from a bottle again. We left the hospital with an NG tube and instructions on how to use it and how to change it. I secretly knew that I would never change it. Many thanks to my wonderful friend, I never had to change it or put it back in when he pulled it out.

But Mommy became the calorie-counting queen. We had to make sure that Brody was still getting enough nutrition without as much formula as a typical baby, so we worked with him at home and in feeding therapy to get him to take things by mouth. At our three-month post-op check-up, the cardiologist was pleased with the results he saw from the surgery and the gains Brody had made in his weight. He told us that we could remove the tube as long as we continued to push him to drink as much as he was willing to consume by mouth. This was a wonderful day.

Today, Brody is a wonderful little boy. I can't believe that he is almost four. He talks and acts silly, just like every other preschooler I know. He loves to meet new people and to talk to them. We saw the cardiologist recently, and he said that Brody is restriction free. He can do anything he wants to do. The most amazing things about Brody are that he is always able to bring a smile to my face, and he gives the best hugs.

A Guiding Constellation
Gina Myers

Gina Myers lives in Southern California with her husband, three daughters, and one son. She enjoys the beach, reading, writing, and cooking. She began volunteering for the Williams Syndrome Association in 2013 as a Regional Coordinator for the Canyon Region.

"By her constellation of heart defects, I would say she has Williams syndrome ... or Noonan. No. Williams."

This is what the cardiologist calmly told me as he still had the ultrasound probe from the echocardiogram in his hand. He went on to explain that my daughter, Rachel, would need heart surgery soon. I asked him how soon, and he responded that it would be as soon as it could be arranged.

And then I was left waiting for blood work to be drawn to confirm the suspected diagnosis. I felt so alone and inevitably began to cry. Rachel 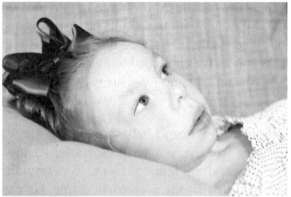 was laying on the gurney, sedated and happily blowing spit bubbles and cooing at the animated aquarium toy that had kept her busy during the test. It felt as if she were worlds away.

In the next few days, Google became my worst enemy as I read everything I could find online. The American Academy of Pediatrics website instilled panic, as we were only a few days away from Rachel's first cardiac catheterization and I read warnings about sudden death from anesthesia. I simply mourned. I took her to have pictures taken and cried the entire time.

I became addicted to one site that featured pictures of kids with Williams syndrome along with their stories. It was hosted by the

University of California at Irvine, which was close to me and made me feel somehow comforted. I memorized the stories and came to know the children by their pictures. As I read their stories over and over again, I began to not feel as alone in this diagnosis.

The results from the cardiac catheterization were very grave—she did need open-heart surgery to repair supravalvular aortic and pulmonary stenosis as soon as possible. We received our positive FISH test results for Williams the day before the surgery. She made it through this surgery and through another to replace her mitral valve just nine months later. She'd had a rough time of it and was left with serious complications as a result of a stroke during surgery. I felt alone once again.

Through all of this, I spoke to a few moms sporadically that I'd been connected with through the early intervention program. They were helpful, but I was overwhelmed and felt that our situation overwhelmed them. My world seemed so very small, consisting of Rachel, who needed me round the clock; my two older daughters; my husband; and my sister-in-law, who had moved in with us to help. Also, I had Rachel's growing number of therapists and doctors. I was grateful for my small circle, but it was isolating too.

By serendipity, a neighbor of ours approached me saying that she worked with someone who had a child with Williams syndrome. Soon, I met another child with Rachel's same diagnosis. So many things made sense! My new friend encouraged me to join Facebook to connect with other Williams syndrome families. Once I did, I was amazed by the wonderful support I found there. It was unconditional—friendships formed fast with this common bond of our children. It was wonderful. Attempting to organize my friends list into categories, I accidentally created the group "WS Support." But I, and many others, realized its potential almost immediately as a safe place to share our problems and triumphs. Now, years later, some of my best friendships are with fellow WS moms whom I have met online.

Rachel has brought me more joy than I'd have ever thought possible. From cherishing her every smile and coo when we thought we would lose her to persevering through the months we spent in the hospital, we tried to take nothing for granted. It feels like a lifetime ago that a doctor told us that we should enjoy the time we had left with her, that she wouldn't survive her complications, and that she would never talk again, would never walk, would never feed herself, and would never lead a normal life.

Now a spunky seven-and-a-half-year-old, Rachel is doing very well! She has surprised all of her doctors with how far she has come. She has survived two open-heart surgeries—against the odds that we were given—and has learned to cope with a movement and seizure disorder. She learned to walk with a walker at first, but within a year and a half, at age four, she was able to beat those odds as well and walk independently. She is a fair eater and loves all things chocolate. She won't even try an ice cream that isn't brown! Of course, she can have bad days, but the good ones outnumber those by far.

She is stubborn and independent, and I think this has contributed to her success. If I call her my baby, she immediately turns and says, "I'm not your baby! I'm your big girl!" When we are out anywhere, she introduces herself to everyone in a loud voice, saying, "Hi, I'm Rachel Myers! What's your name? What are you doing here?" She is interested in everyone. To her, everyone is a potential friend. I am always surprised by the kindness she elicits from those she meets. I try so hard to intercept her spontaneous hugs to strangers, but often she is just too fast for me! In her eyes, everyone deserves a hug.

Whenever I look into my daughter's beautiful eyes, I am reminded of what the cardiologist told me, the strange phrase that he used—that my daughter had a "constellation" of defects. I look into the starburst pattern in her eyes and see a universe within. I look out into my relationships within the WS community and see another universe there—all points of light that wouldn't exist for me without my daughter. She guides me as I guide her.

To "No Fear"

You found us as we smiled
through the crowd eager to meet another version
of our own daughter
It was our first time
there
at the Salk, the 2010 Mardi Gras Williams Picnic

You asked me, "Why does she have that?"

Pointing to her ever-present walker, and staring frankly at my three-
year-old daughter
"She needs extra help to walk," I said automatically

"Oh," you said, leaving
But soon came back, your beautiful blue eyes brimming with tears
Then you addressed my daughter, my Rachel, directly:
"You must walk. You will walk. You must come back and be one of
us."
"One of us, you hear."

And when the parade ended, the drums, tambourines, and clappers
stopped
Singers silenced, and the young ones comforted and quieted
You found us once more

You looked into Rachel's eyes, blue like yours
Pointed resolutely to your arm
And to the fresh temporary tattoo affixed there
"No Fear," you said.
"No Fear, you see."
"No Fear."

Rachel is walking now
in spite of what doctors might have said
called her ballistic
dismissed her
Forgot …

But we do not.
Thank you, No Fear,
We hope to see you again.

Photo credit: Natalie Mzrotek

That's Our Max

Mandy Keep

Mandy Keep lives in Collegeville, Pennsylvania. She has two children and enjoys reading, writing, and photography.

Max is two years old and is just about to start preschool two days a week. Born in April 2010, Max was diagnosed with Williams syndrome in July 2011. After detecting a heart murmur at three months old, his pediatrician referred us to the Cardiology Department at duPont Hospital for Children.

Max had a 100 percent successful open-heart surgery for supravalvular aortic stenosis in May of 2013 at duPont, and doctors were astonished at his speedy recovery in both the Intensive Care Unit and regular recovery room. Max had to be on bypass for two days after his operation to let it rest and, once his heart was back to beating on its own, there was no stale day after that. After nine or ten days, he was released. We haven't had any problems since, and we received a clean bill of health from the doctors. Max loves to bounce everywhere, and he loves his younger brother Gage (most of the time—he does have his moments), who is sixteen months old. We are thankful to have Gage to help Max along from now through years to come.

Max is an inspiration and a joy to everyone he meets. He is a social butterfly whose favorite words are "hi" and "bye-bye!" To look at him, you wouldn't know he had gone through something so traumatic months ago. Today he is receiving top-notch coaching and guidance from early intervention services in terms of occupational therapy, physical therapy,

special instruction, speech therapy, behavioral therapy, and vision therapy. All of these therapies have been 100 percent beneficial to his development. Max is able to complete simple puzzles independently, such as squares, circles, triangles, and animals. We are using picture schedules and social stories. He enjoys reading books and turning the pages on request. He likes playing simple group games and loves music like "Ring Around the Rosie," which makes him smile.

Physical therapy helped Max start walking at eighteen months. Every week, he would double his steps and made us very proud. Now he's climbing the stairs by holding the rail comfortably by himself. Vision therapy is helping him with things such as tracking objects, placing colored tape on stairs inside and outside of the home, and using a light box to highlight objects. Max likes going out into the community to places such as the library and the park and going to playdates with the peers he's known since he was a baby.

Max has developed excellent fine motor skills, listens to directions most of the time, is starting to have good manners ("more, please," "thank you," blowing kisses) and has good attention and focus for most activities. Max has a lot of need for sensory input and also has some sensitivity to loud sounds. We help this by regular massage and by listening to and watching online videos. He is also spoiled by having a one-hundred pound trampoline in the living room. He is infatuated with opening and closing doors and by the repetition of putting things into and taking them out of a bag or box. He'd rather push a stroller or bike than ride on it. We only had to change two therapists in the past because the relationship and techniques they tried weren't working well with Max. He'd refuse to take part and get very upset. The change brought fresh, playful, and fun activities during these sessions.

We are currently getting Max evaluated with Indian Creek Foundation for behavioral health for Wraparound Services because of his limited expressive language, our concerns with his tantrums, and some worrying aggressive behavior to himself and toward his brother. When Max gets into trouble, it's usually because of a health issue going on like constipation, reflux, needing to burp, or headaches. Sometimes he struggles when he doesn't have anything in his hands. He does have a little mean streak in him. That's where the expressive language piece will help us all when he can tell us the problem versus crying, having a temper tantrum, or hitting his brother.

As far as Max's diet, he eats like a horse! He loves blueberry pie, Marie Callender's turkey dinners, donuts (which he calls "dough"), and coconut water daily. We give him lots of fruits and veggies, salmon, and other fish a couple of times a week. He also takes a fish oil supplement every day to help his brain and heart, vitamin E in moderation, and bilberry to strengthen his eye muscles. We use lavender essential oil to help ease Max's pain and to focus on issues that he might be experiencing. We also use eucalyptus and melatonin at night to help him sleep more soundly. (He isn't on any other medication.) His supplements are all natural, and we have seen a lot of progress with this routine. He is very aware of his surroundings. He gets a little overwhelmed on some occasions, but his stamina and determination are through the roof. I am sure Max will make a great athlete someday and will take after his mommy, who always likes to win!

Rocky Road
Ivy Weesner

Ivy lives in Phoenix, Arizona with her hubby and three kids. She loves to play softball, hike, swim, write, and raise their mini urban farm.

Oakley Mae Grace, also appropriately known as OMG, was born in January of 2007. My pregnancy with her was a breeze. I had gained over forty pounds with both of my other pregnancies, but with Oakley I gained only a whopping eighteen pounds. While that can be very healthy, in hindsight it would be the first of many rocks we would trip over, kick, or climb in the pathway of Oakley's life.

Oakley was delivered in a planned C-section and was full term; however, the doctor was disappointed with her size—six pounds and seven ounces. She came out with *huge,* dark purple lips and screamed like a kitty with her tail slammed in the door. She was rushed to the

NICU for oxygen, where she stayed briefly and was deemed "feisty" in big letters on her chart. After that, she was attached to me like we had never been separated. My baby girl was never content. If she would sleep, it was only on my chest. Her early days were spent screaming, rocking, and pacing.

She soon developed an umbilical hernia the size of a fat thumb. Umbilical hernias are common, so we didn't worry until one day it turned black and as hard as a rock. A doctor said there was a 1 percent chance it could get strangulated, at which point it would become an emergency because within minutes it would kill the tissue that was caught. It took us half a dozen trips to the emergency room to get them to take us seriously. When it would get strangulated, I would literally pop it back in, rush her in, sit, and wait until they would look at it and tell me it was fine. I know they thought I was crazy to be freaked out over a hernia, so I decided to just sit in the parking lot and wait until the moment that it was black and hard again, when I would dash in the door and throw her in front of the check-in nurse. You wouldn't believe the response I got then! It took three nurses and a doctor to pop it back in. I think I even offered to help. At eight weeks old, she was put in surgery to repair it. We had hoped that would solve the screaming, but to no avail. This was our second rock in the road of many to come.

Oakley became more content the older she got, but we still, to this day, struggle with getting her to sleep. She quit napping when she was very young. We also couldn't get her to gain weight. She ate and ate and ate but never got anywhere. At three years old, she looked like a starving child. She wasn't even on the growth chart, became severely anemic, and had a hard potbelly, puny arms, and black circles under her eyes. She spent most nights in the bathroom—constipated, vomiting, and miserable. She was poked and prodded by doctors trying to determine what she was lacking, but we didn't have an answer until a family reunion where an aunt looked at her closely for five minutes and proclaimed, "Why, as sure as it is humid in Kansas, this one is a celiac." She was right. We removed gluten from her diet so that her body could absorb nutrients, and in the next year, she grew over three inches in height, four shoe sizes, and ten pounds. We were on-our-knees grateful! It was another rock we didn't have to clumsily stumble over anymore.

Oakley developed on the back end of the range. She waited a long time to talk, but when she did, it was masterful! We also noticed how social she was at a very young age—so much so that we didn't let very many people take her anywhere because she disappeared quickly. Say the word *sticker*, *sucker*, or *shiny,* and you have her undivided attention. I've naturally been pretty protective of her, which has only progressed. We use a lot of caution when we go anywhere with her. We always say, "If you wanna make friends at a party, bring Oakley. Just make sure you know where she is!" This road may never be smooth.

Other small pebbles in our path include an ambulance ride at eighteen months old to the hospital. She had dark purple limbs all the way up to her trunk! The doctors suspected a heart condition but, after a follow-up, they found nothing. She continues to turn a little blue when it's cold, so she owns quite a few pairs of footed jammies!

And a little while later, she was tested for early development. It was no surprise that her language skills were off-the-chart awesome. Her logic, reasoning, and anything cognitive were very low. I was concerned, though I didn't yet realize just how big a boulder I was still climbing.

When Oakley was three and a half years old, a friend met her at a party and wrote me so sweetly. She said that Oakley reminded her of a friend's daughter; that they looked and acted like twins. She mentioned that her friend's daughter had Williams syndrome, but she was so discreet, or I was so thick, that I didn't put it together. I think I wrote back something like, "They do look alike!" Several months later, we went to a wedding that this same friend attended. She specifically sought out Oakley to interact with and then wrote me again, apologetically, but expressing that she really thought I should look into it. Her courage knocked me off my feet—as did what I would find!

Needless to say, Oakley was tested for Williams syndrome when she was four years old, and the test came back positive.

Oakley is our caretaker, our mercy giver, our compassionate friend. She is extremely sensitive to others and incredibly precious to everyone she meets. I wouldn't change a thing about her. I want to be more like her! We don't want any sympathy because we know we've been given a gift. And as for the rocks in our road—well, a little off-roading is good for the soul. So we continue to walk the road less traveled, hand-in-hand.

Our Special Birthday Surprise
Melissa Felsher

Melissa Felsher has a daughter, Josie. She lives in Manhattan on the Upper East Side and loves everything about New York City.

A fortieth birthday is always a big milestone in a person's life. For me, it provided a gift that would last a lifetime—the gift of our daughter, Josie Emerson Portnoy, six pounds, seven ounces. It had been an easy and joyful pregnancy, with one exception. At my twenty-week sonogram, I was told that only one kidney had formed so far but that it appeared to be healthy and normal. Fluid levels were fine, but they would have to watch me very closely. As a family court lawyer, I need to be strong for the people I represent in some heartbreaking situations, but upon hearing this news, I admit I was devastated. The doctors, our family, and friends reassured us that she would be fine. After all, many people with one kidney went on to live totally normal lives. I met with a pediatric urologist before Josie was even born. I went for weekly sonograms, embarking on a life (without knowing it at the time) that would soon be filled with specialists and many, many doctors.

Josie was an easy baby from the start. She ate and slept well. She only cried when it was time to eat. When she was three weeks old, her pediatrician heard a slight heart murmur and said something to me that I had not yet heard. He explained that he was going to send us to Cardiology because "sometimes heart and kidney issues go together." This was very surprising. At that early cardiology visit, there were some irregularities in her exam, and we were told to come back when she was three months old because "if there was going to be a narrowing, it would be evident by then." Again, this comment didn't mean anything to us at the time, but in hindsight it became clear. The doctors were already thinking, *Williams syndrome*.

Josie continued to develop as she should, meeting her early milestones. She was sleeping and eating beautifully, so we gave little thought to the upcoming three-month cardiology visit. We were completely astounded when we received the information at the appointment that changed our lives. After the EKG and echocardiogram, the cardiologist took out a pen and started drawing the heart valves on a piece of paper. She was talking about a narrowing in a valve above the aorta, but as her words were humming through my head, I couldn't breathe and I couldn't focus. She told me that she wanted to call Genetics to do a FISH test. It was the first time I heard the words "Williams syndrome." I would soon come to know the words "supravalvular aortic stenosis" and "Williams syndrome" extremely well.

The week waiting for the results of the genetic test was excruciating. I looked up "Williams syndrome" online and thought it just couldn't be.

Josie was not the infant they were describing. She wasn't colicky. She didn't have difficulty eating or sleeping. When the results were confirmed, I sank into a deep depression. I looked at this tiny baby whom I loved and thought, *I didn't sign up for this. I don't want a lifetime of this.* I immediately sought out professional help to assist me in getting through this dark period. A few weeks later, after I mourned the loss of the child I thought I would have, I pulled myself together and, like the aggressive lawyer inside me, I sprang into action and have not looked back.

Josie started with early intervention services when she was a mere five months old, and her vigorous therapeutic schedule has continued ever since. Developmentally, I am grateful to say that Josie is doing extremely well. She has always met all her milestones within the time frame for typically developing children. She has always been mainstreamed at school and has many friendships.

There have been more bumps medically. Her repertoire of doctors is vast. At two years old, she had surgery to correct bladder reflux. At three and a half years old, she had open-heart surgery to repair her SVAS.

Recently, Josie started medication for high blood pressure due to a structural abnormality in her descending aorta. With each surgery and round of tests to get to the root of a problem, I struggle. For the two months before her open-heart surgery, I walked around consumed with her impending surgery, unable to understand how the rest of the world was carrying on, laughing, and living, when my little girl was having such massive surgery. For me, because I take these things so hard, it has been an up-and-down ride emotionally.

There are regular and frequent appointments with all her specialists: cardiology, urology, nephrology. Josie has worn blood pressure monitors, had MRIs and MRAs. But these are not the things that define Josie. Josie is a tireless warrior. She is a rock star! And that is what defines her. And it is those qualities in Josie that help me to remember to breathe and also have enabled me to handle much more than I ever thought possible.

In the time since her diagnosis at just a few months old, we have learned with certainty that we got more than we could have asked for. After five shared birthdays, Josie is, and always will be, my greatest gift. She fills our lives with light and brightness. Josie hugs tightly, shrieks with excitement loudly, laughs and plays wholly, tries and succeeds mightily, shines brightly, and loves fully!

Happy birthday to us!

Part II

Life Goes On—
Beautifully

Chapter 3

Sports

When we first learn about Williams syndrome, it seems that we almost inherently focus on the limitations—what those who have it will not be able to do or will be lacking. But as time goes on and milestone after milestone is met, those limitations become fewer and fewer for most, and we learn that assuming anything to be out of reach is senseless. Instead, focusing on what can *be achieved, even with low muscle tone and a host of other "limiting" characteristics, proves to be a much more rewarding practice.*

Swim, Ashley, Swim

Cathy Kohlun

Cathy Kohlun has three children, Chris, Courtney, and Ashley, who has Williams syndrome. She has been married to her husband, Bruce, for forty-two years and has three grandsons and a granddaughter. A retired high school English teacher, Cathy lives in Norman, Oklahoma, and loves scrapbooking, photography, and traveling.

It was time for swim lessons. Ashley's brother, Chris, and her sister, Courtney, were enrolled—so Ashley was going too. We had tried when she was ten months and at ages two, three, and four, usually quitting after a day or two of crying and deciding she wasn't ready. This time, she was five. She immediately jumped into the arms of the cute college instructor. He had her swimming within days. I guess it was the right person, or simply the right moment in time.

When Ashley turned six, she entered her first swim meet. At age eight, she swam in her first Special Olympics swim meet. She came in second because she stopped to let the other girls catch up with her. When she realized she had earned a silver medal, she said next time she was going to wait on the other side of the pool for the girls so she could get the gold medal. This was just the beginning of her swimming career. She had found her way to shine.

Ashley was a natural in the water. Her favorite stroke was the breaststroke. She was unbeatable. At fourteen, we nominated her for the Special Olympics World Games held in 1995. After she was selected and spent a year training intensively, she won five medals, including the prestigious gold. She was a star!

Ashley started high school after returning from World Games. Her coach wanted Ashley to continue her training for future games, but after she met with her high school's swim team coach and he saw her swim, Ashley joined the high school swim team. Ashley was thrilled, but I was concerned about what might happen. As a high school teacher, I *knew* what could happen! However, we knew we had to allow our little fish to swim.

Ashley was now a Norman Tiger! We were all very proud of her, although I was concerned with the level of competition, and Ashley was used to winning. How would she handle this new world? Would the other swimmers accept her? Could she keep up? Ashley had no doubt. She thrived. She had to ride a bus from the high school to the university pool every day. She loved every minute of it, including a bus full of athletes to talk to.

She practiced six days per week—five high school practices and one Special Olympics practice. She swam in every meet that year, always coming in last place. Everyone was very proud of her. I held my breath a lot. There were times I wondered if we had made the right decision. As the qualified swimmers prepared for the state meet, I had a talk with her to see how she was feeling about the team and the competition level.

During our talk, I asked her how she felt about coming in last place, but I couldn't say the words. She was silent, and I was worried. Finally, she said, "Mom, I usually come in last. You've been to all the meets. I always come in last!" My heart stopped—she knew. I wasn't sure she realized it.

"My coach tells me you have to be a really good swimmer to be on the Norman High swim team, and I am!" she said. "He tells the other swimmers that I have had a race shown on ESPN, and none of them have and may never have one. Mom, you know I am in training for Special Olympics and I will get my medals there, so don't worry. One more thing, the team needs my 4.0 grade point average. How do you think that *we* won the All-State Academic Medal?"

Ashley remained on the team. As a sophomore, she was a substitute on a relay team and *didn't* come in last place on several races. She was called on to race in a 4 x 50 freestyle relay race. She went off the block and swam great! The team came in second place. She continued practicing and preparing for Special Olympics. Her success continued each year as she placed higher in more races. As a senior, she told her coach that this was an important year because she was going to the World Games again after graduation. And she worked harder than ever. She placed ninth out of sixteen in the Mid-State meet that year, just missing the cut for the state meet.

The 1999 Special Olympics World Games were held in North Carolina. Ashley came home with many medals. She went on to the Special Olympics National Games in 2010. Now, she says she has too many medals to count and hopes to attend more national and world games in the future. She tells people her greatest accomplishment so far was being a Norman Tiger because it gave her a chance to show others that you can be successful if you put your mind to it.

Ashley and I discussed several possible stories to submit to this book. She asked me to tell this one because she wants parents to help their children find things to participate in. She doesn't want parents to be afraid to let their children try. She says that kids need to figure out how to get along in the world. Ashley has very good insight and has had many wonderful experiences. She is an inspiration to others in our community. As difficult as it was on us as parents to let her try, we hoped it was the best for her, and she says it was!

The Prom
Debbie Payne

How do I express twenty years of loving my son and all the wonderful stories into so few words? How do I pick just one story? Impossible. Jacob adds so much meaning and joy to our lives. My husband, two other sons, and I are so grateful that he is part of our family.

When Jake was diagnosed at three, we were heartbroken. At each stage, I would wonder how we would get through—from the screaming and projectile vomiting, to looking for the wandering child in Walmart, to the battles of learning math and penmanship. Yes, I miss those days, and you will too. I am not sure why we were so upset eighteen years ago with the diagnosis. I cannot imagine a day in my life without him in it.

I am so thankful to the moms with children with Williams syndrome who answered my calls (pre-Internet!) for the first year or so and did not laugh at silly questions like, "Will Jake go to the prom?" They were my lifeline to sanity!

Jacob is kind, funny, and a bit stubborn. When he was five, he wanted a dirt bike so badly but refused to even try to ride a two-wheeler with training wheels. He was very happy racing down the driveway on the Big Wheel. We told him he could have a dirt bike only if he could ride the bike. I'll be … He came inside on a snowy January afternoon and said he was ready to buy a dirt bike. He had taught himself to ride! He said the snow made it not hurt when he fell (it apparently had nothing to do with all the snow clothes). By spring he was riding a little 50 dirt bike.

We never made excuses for Jake. His brothers played sports, and so did he. He played soccer and baseball with the local recreation council. When he was about eight, I spoke with the commissioners, and they let him play with an age group below his for a couple more years. It worked out perfectly! His brothers were in Scouts, and so was he. Jake made it through Cub Scouts and earned all the pins and the Arrow of Light. If there was something special he was interested in, like Junior Firefighters, he joined. He now is a member of Hereford Volunteer Fire Company and is in the Knights of Columbus at church.

Jake started high school in 2007, right after the movie *Super Bad* was released. He was instantly tagged as "McLovin," a name he is still called six years later—"Chica chica yeah yeah …" He played Allied Sports (soccer, bowling and softball) in high school all four years. He was a Baltimore County Outstanding Athlete and, in his senior year, he was named Athlete of the Year. (This award was for an athlete from all of sports at Hereford; he ousted even the future collegiate lacrosse, wrestling, and track athletes!) That stubbornness to achieve was rewarded. Now, he participates in Special Olympics in both track and distance cycling and loves it.

Our family has learned to appreciate the smallest accomplishments and the simplest acts of kindness. We are free to laugh at ourselves, and we try not to sweat the small stuff. I really think that Jake's brothers are who they are in part because of Jake. Rob, the older brother, wanted to stand out, so he took up magic at a young age. He now performs for audiences of all ages and wants a career directing and producing movies. Kev, the younger brother, set himself apart in athletics. He enjoys coaching track for Special Olympics. You may have seen him. He has been at the last several conventions watching the babies. He is also planning a cross-country bike ride in 2014 to raise awareness for the Williams Syndrome Association.

Years ago, a mom of a newly diagnosed toddler expressed fear of having baby number two. My response was, "In my opinion, that is the best way to teach her to share and fight fairly in a safe environment." I so clearly remember trying to teach my boys the tradition of sacrificing something for Lent, to give something up for only forty days. Jake was about seven, and his response was, "I'll give up fighting with my brothers—unless they start it." It made sense, but I think we encouraged him to give up Tootsie Rolls instead.

I often forget that Jake's world is very literal. Once, we were at the beach; he may have been about four (looking about two). He said he had to "pee." The thought of packing everyone up and carrying three boys across the hot sand and boardwalk to get to the hotel was just too much. I told him just to pee in the ocean. After all, whales pee in the ocean. Before I could even get up from building the sandcastle, Jake ran down *near* the water, dropped his suit to his ankles, and proceeded … Everyone on the beach, including the lifeguards, just roared. What could I do but laugh?

All of you who have a child over four or five know that trying to teach a child to do chores is a chore in and of itself. Well, it was one of those days when just one more thing would have sent me over the edge. I had asked Jake time and time again to clean his room. I finally said something to the effect of, "Will you just do *something*!" and his reply was, "I *am* doing something. I am waiting for a friend to call." *He* told *me*! I can laugh at that story now.

Fast forward to today—Jacob is healthy, happy, and productive. Isn't that what we want for *any* of our children? He has worked at Wegmans' grocery store for over a year. What a great employer! He goes to the movies almost every Friday night with a friend after work. And, of course, he still enjoys riding a four-wheeler and dirt bike and tearing up the fields.

Jake's other passion is taking care of his animals. He expressed a desire to care for cows, so he talked to a local farmer and bought two calves last spring. It is Jake's responsibility to go out and feed Corby and Bess every day, to check their water, and to walk the fence line to be sure it is secure. He is not a huge fan of the electric fence, so he learned quickly how to turn it off to fix any breaks!

Oh, I almost forgot! Jacob went to the prom. As a matter of fact, just as Nancy had predicted about fourteen years before, he went to so many proms that it made sense to buy him a tux. For most proms he had a date; for one he went stag. When he went to the prom alone, he took three dozen gerbera daisies to give to the beautiful ladies. He had so much fun dancing with everyone and came away from prom with two phone numbers and several new Facebook friends. "Chica chica yeah yeah!"

Enjoy your little ones in every stage. If you are anything like me, you will miss all those fleeting moments in time!

Fifty Frozen Cokes to Bike Riding
Michelle Self and Bill Bentley

Bill and Michelle live in Ohio and have two boys, Bill and Alex. Bill is a nuclear engineer, and Michelle is an education consultant helping others to break down tasks and get the educational help they need. She is also currently on the WSA Board of Trustees.

Alex was diagnosed with Williams syndrome when he was six weeks old. We read the pamphlets and went to the Williams Syndrome Association website. We found a lot of information about the types of things that Alex would probably not be able to do, but we also knew that, despite the typical expectations, Alex was his own person. We didn't know what he might be capable of, and we certainly weren't going to hold him back.

Alex learned to walk when he was two years old. With a lot of help and physical therapy, he rode a tricycle and then a bike with training wheels. Our family likes to go on bike rides, so when Alex finished kindergarten it was time for him to join in the fun. It wasn't going to be easy, but we decided our summer project would be to teach our seven-year-old how to ride a bike.

Step one was to get Alex a bike that he could sit on but have his feet reach the ground so he could easily hold it up. Step two was to drive Alex and his bike to a nice, big, open park where he could have lots of room with nothing to run into. At first, Alex learned that he could just push the bike along with his feet—no problem. Then came the big step, moving forward and pedaling without falling. Dad had to follow along and hold Alex up for a lot of attempts. Then, little by little, Dad was holding on less and less. After a while, and with a nice big push start from Dad, Alex was pedaling along all on his own!

Did Alex fall sometimes? Of course. Did Alex get discouraged and want to quit? Of course. But we kept practicing every day, and Alex had lots of motivation to reach that goal. We kept reminding him that he could ride his bike to his friends' houses, especially the little girl down the street whom he liked so much. If he learned how to ride, then he could join his older brother and us for rides around the neighborhood. But best of all, if he would practice for twenty minutes, then we would take him for a frozen Coke. Alex loves frozen Cokes. Plus, nothing makes a pair of scratched-up knees feel better than the taste of a frosty frozen Coke.

So we kept going to the park and giving him frozen Cokes. Anytime he got upset with us, afterward he would say, "I'm so sorry, Mom and Dad. I know you are doing what's best." After Alex learned to pedal his bike, we then had to teach him how to stop. First, he would stop by just falling off the bike, and then he would stop by dragging his feet. He literally wore holes in the bottoms of his tennis shoes. We would tell him, "Alex, you're not Fred Flintstone. Use your bike brakes!" It took him a while to get used to pushing the pedal in reverse to brake, but after some more frozen Cokes, he got it.

The last step was learning how to take off on his own. Dad wasn't going to be there all the time to give Alex his big push to get him started. This took some more practice and some more frozen Cokes. At first, Alex used the "rolling start" method—he would get himself moving with his feet and then shift to pedaling. But eventually he figured out how to hold himself up on the bike and push off on the pedals to get moving on his own. How many frozen Cokes in all did it take that summer? Maybe fifty, maybe more.

Alex is thirteen years old now. We have taken countless bike rides around our community. We are talking about taking a bike tour sometime in the future. Alex continues to amaze us with what he can do every day. We don't worry about the things that Alex can't do. We just try to make sure that Alex has the chance to do as many activities that he would enjoy as possible. He has played on a soccer team, sung solos on a stage, auditioned for and made his junior high school show choir, volunteered with many organizations through church, and many other things. The other day, Alex and I were driving somewhere in the car, and he looked over and said, "I have a pretty good life." I asked him why, and he said, "I am doing good in school. I'm in the talent show and show choir. I help people. I think it is pretty good." How can you argue with that?

The Benefit of Basketball
Niki Gilmore

Like most children with Williams syndrome, AJ was very young when he developed a fascination for "spinning" things. He would spin the wheels on his toy cars and spin balls on the floor. Around age three he began dribbling a basketball, and by age ten he was spinning it on his finger quite well. However, his preferred school activity has always been band. He has played the violin using the Suzuki method since first grade. He is now in eighth grade and still plays the violin. He has the only stringed instrument in the entire school! He still has no idea how to read music. His band teacher is very impressed with AJ's ability to learn to play everything only by sound. He also plays the keyboard quite well after only five lessons from a local music store.

He never showed an interest in either joining a basketball team or shooting hoops until middle school, when some of AJ's friends from band mentioned trying out for the basketball team. He was beaming! He has had a hoop at home since he was twelve and does a great job at sinking the ball but had never shown an interest in joining a team. It was all he talked about for a month. He came home every day and practiced. We tried to teach him the rules of the game; however, things like traveling and which direction to go down the court seemed confusing.

AJ tried out for the team every day after school for one week. The following week, AJ told us he had made the junior varsity team! He was given a jersey and went to every practice and game. AJ's coach, Gillian, said he never saw a kid light up so much with a jersey on. He put AJ in every game for about five minutes. By the time he was back on the bench, we could see the relief on his face. He had that "deer in the headlights" look when he was on the court. He still, however, told us at the beginning of every game, "I'm going to win this game for you!"

At the very last game, the coach had AJ step into the middle of the court for the coin toss. The cheerleaders started chanting, "Let's go, AJ! Let's go!" Other teammates, students, and parents chimed in as well. He was so focused on the game that he seemed a bit oblivious to how wonderful it was. I sat on the sidelines choked up and in tears with pride for my son. Being a part of a team, like being a part of the band, has been such a positive experience for AJ. He has developed a great sense of pride in himself. He is now fourteen and still feels like a superstar at school. We took AJ to a Charlotte Bobcats basketball game, which further fueled his interest and love for the game. He wants to play on the team next year in high school and continues to practice after school almost every day.

AJ is mainstreamed into regular classes for the first time this year in eighth grade. He is quite a popular teenager with the entire support of the school. You would never know he is at a second-grade reading level and first-grade math level. He is able to pick up some of the information in the regular education classroom just by being included. Homework has been challenging, and we have had to remove all game systems (iPad, PS3, etc.) from his life because he lost interest in everything he loved when video games were allowed. We also have had a tutor every Saturday for the last three years to get him to where he is today. His social skills have improved tenfold this year, and we think much of that comes from being a basketball player! We have hopes that high school will be just as successful and that he will still love to go every day.

AJ has a sister, Alexis, who has been very patient with him as well. She is now eighteen, enjoys taking him to the mall and movies, and also seems less discouraged with him and his lack of abilities. AJ has an incredible love for music, fishing, yo-yos, dancing and basketball. We couldn't be more proud to have an individual with Williams syndrome in our lives!

Cheerleader Not Afraid to Live Her Dream

Shirley Parrell

Shirley Parrell lives in New Jersey with her husband, Jeff, and children Emily, Laura, and John.

Laura began cheering when she was eight years old and in the third grade. Ever since she was five years old, she asked her cardiologist if she could get clearance to participate. After years of pleading, she finally broke him down and immediately joined a cheer squad. She participated on a typical squad with her peers in competitive cheering. The season began on the first Monday of August, and by October of the very first year, all the staff at her elementary school were commenting about how much more confident they found Laura to be. Cheering was her life! Each time she was asked to complete a written assignment, she chose only two topics: her love for cheering and helping the younger girls.

Kaitlin Fallucca, during her first year as a head coach, had Laura on her team. This was Laura's third year of cheering, and she was at level

three. When Kaitlin's team took first place at the regional competition, the regional officials asked her to write about her first year as a coach and any cheerleaders she thought motivated the team. When Kaitlin told me about the request, I was overjoyed for her. She then said, "No, you're not getting it. I'm writing about Laura." I was speechless.

When I first saw the article, I was brought to tears. I was so amazed that this young coach "got it." I was impressed that she wasn't annoyed or "put out" by having Laura on her team. Laura can be a handful, and there are cheering moves that can be challenging for her. This just shows that kids with Williams syndrome can compete and participate on teams with their typical peers. It also goes to show that there are coaches who understand that our kids just want to be accepted, and some coaches will also recognize how our kids can use their gifts to help the team. Kaitlin is overjoyed to have you read her story about my daughter below:

Laura was born with two different heart problems. One is pulmonary stenosis (the artery going to her lungs is smaller and narrower than it should be), and the second is mild mitral valve prolapse (the flaps that open and close to let blood into the heart are abnormally stretchy, creating a minor leak). Despite these conditions, Laura has more heart than most.

When Laura was six, she was diagnosed with Williams syndrome. This is a rare genetic condition that occurs in about 1 in 10,000 births. People born with Williams syndrome have a deletion on chromosome seven. Williams syndrome can be characterized by cardiovascular disease, developmental delays, and learning disabilities. Meeting Laura, you would not realize any of this, but it certainly makes life harder for her.

Even still, Laura is a happy child that will be the first to volunteer to help with anything you need. She may appear to be average, but she is far from it. When your "average" cheerleader gets a common cold, chances are that she will take an over the counter medication and skip practices to rest. Laura cannot take any cold medicine, only a simple cough drop. However, sick or not, she did not miss a single practice all season. That changed when the doctors diagnosed Laura with yet a third heart problem this year.

Immediately after the diagnosis, Laura was unable to participate with the team for some time. Instead of sulking in the corner watching her team practice without her or skipping practice altogether, Laura became proactive. She attended every practice of our flag squad and mentored them from the sidelines. She was a tremendous help with the little ones, even from a chair, and when it was time for the local competition, the flag team performed wonderfully. Although Laura could not actually participate at the local competition with her team, she cried more tears of joy than anyone else when her team won first place. It seems like there is nothing wrong with Laura's heart!

Laura was medically cleared immediately after the local competition. She didn't miss a beat. She worked hard to make up for all of the practices she missed. Her team placed first at Metro Qualifiers, as well as Eastern Regionals. Laura is now part of our club's history, as her team was the first to go to Nationals to compete at Disney World. Her proudest moment was getting to pose with Mickey in the winner's picture!

Although her mother has a four-inch binder full of Laura's medical history, Laura keeps going. Despite heart problems, a genetic disorder, or anything else that gets in her way, Laura has a love for cheering. For those of you afraid to live your dream, take a step back and think of Laura!

The third heart issue Laura was diagnosed with was prolonged QT syndrome. There was about a month that she was sidelined from all activity including gym class, other recreational activities, and running. For many days, she was attached to both twenty-four and forty-eight hour leads, when finally the doctors were able to figure out the correct level of beta-blocker that she needed. She was allowed to go back to her regular activities with some restrictions.

Laura moved to a higher age group, and this team came in first at Regionals and also competed in Nationals at Disney World. The cheerleading club was a great second family for Laura. The entire coaching staff loved Laura and pushed her to participate as fully as she was allowed. She made many friends and continues to cherish her memories as a member of the cheerleading teams.

Since then, our family moved to a town that offers a more challenging academic program for Laura. Her academics and independence have thrived in our new district. Unfortunately, they do not offer a cheerleading program. Laura is presently in the eighth grade and plans on trying out for the high school cheer squad next year. She is currently using her "free" time to explore tennis and horseback riding.

My Delaney: Our Firstborn, Our Only Girl, and Forever Our Princess

Heather L. O'Connell

Heather lives in New Jersey with her husband, Tim, and three children, Delaney, Kyle, and Jake. She runs a Special Olympics program for a variety of sports, coaches ice hockey, owns a photography business, is a regional chair for the WSA, and has been newly appointed to the Mercer County Board of Mental Health.

Five months into my first pregnancy, we learned that our little girl would be born with a very rare heart condition called Ebstein's anomaly. All the joy that comes with having your first child turned into fear and anxiety. She was born in June of 2002 and had a much shorter stay at Children's Hospital of Philadelphia than expected. All

the doctors kept telling us what a miracle and fighter she was. It was very surreal. Once home, her development did not go as it should have and by one year old, Delaney was diagnosed with Williams syndrome.

I think as most families do, we grieved. We grieved because becoming new parents to a little girl had not gone as we thought it would. But so much of Delaney now made sense. We kicked life into full gear and sought out therapies and specialists. Our goal now was to give our princess the best we could. We wanted her to be the most successful that she could be in life.

There are so many great stories I could tell you about Delaney, but I want to share our experience with Special Olympics New Jersey and the incredible impact it has had on our family of five.

When Delaney was three, we found the Young Athletes Program at Special Olympics New Jersey. We are very lucky that the New Jersey headquarters is in the town next to ours. Delaney started to participate in the Young Athletes Program. We went on Saturday mornings, and she was able to work on gross motor skills while we met other parents with children with special needs. As our two boys, Kyle and Jake, were born and grew older, they were able to participate too. We really had a wonderful time on Saturday mornings. Delaney also participated in the Young Athletes Program at the Summer Games. This really opened our eyes to what Special Olympics could mean for our princess. It was a place where she could belong and feel a great sense of pride. To see athletes with special needs older than myself enjoying life and being so successful was just what we really needed to see.

When Delaney turned eight, she became eligible to do so much more with Special Olympics. I started coaching track for a local community Special Olympics New Jersey team, and Delaney began to make friends, become more physically fit, and feel a sense of pride in herself. I push Delaney athletically. I push her as her mother and as her coach. I push her because I know she can do it.

What an amazing choice I made to coach Special Olympics. I do it for Delaney, but I also do it for myself. I also coach ice hockey in a regular ice hockey league for my youngest, Jake. I have coached my boys' T-ball team also. But I am most drawn to coaching athletes with special needs. These are kids who can do, who work hard, and who share immense joy in their accomplishments. They *give* such joy.

But back to my princess. We had our first area meet, which then took us to the Summer Games. The sheer joy on Delaney's face when she got on the stand, winning her first medal ever, was something I'll never forget. In 2010, Delaney and I participated in our first ever Summer Games. I thought it was very cool that my second-grader was going to live in a dorm on campus at The College of New Jersey for the weekend. What Delaney thought was so cool was all the people she got to meet, such as all the state troopers lined up in the stadium to greet the athletes and give high fives as they marched in for opening ceremonies. She also loved listening to the live band on the football field and sitting with her teammates and friends to watch fireworks after the cauldron was lit to signal the start of the Summer Games. The next day, when the text messages flew in about her picture on the front page of the newspaper with a Rutgers football player, she felt like the celebrity she always wanted to be.

As a mother and a coach, I was nervous on our first day of competition. But not my Delaney. All her fans had come out to see her. She wanted to win. She wanted medals. By the end of the weekend, she had three medals to her name. We knew this was just the beginning. Seeing the pride on my daughter's face when she went into school with all her medals was such a wonderful moment.

Delaney's first year playing Special Olympics basketball was trying. She would cry every time her team lost. They were a young team and losing happened often, but they made it to the spring festival in Wildwood that year, and her team won gold! She also participates in soccer and noncompetitive ice skating, although she would like to do that competitively.

Delaney has been to three Summer Games, a spring festival, a fall festival, Camp Shriver, and the American Girl Fashion Show, which is a fund-raiser for Special Olympics New Jersey.

At the 2012 Summer Games, Delaney was asked to introduce the Global Messenger at a reception prior to opening ceremonies. There were a few hundred people there. She was given a speech to read, which we practiced at home and at school. She was so excited. Any time Delaney is given an opportunity to get on a stage and use a microphone, she becomes the most confident person I know. She was amazing! She was spot on with her speech, even interacting with the audience when appropriate. I could not believe the poise that my just-turned-ten-year-old had. I was so proud and also jealous because I still get nervous speaking in front of a crowd, and she made it look so easy.

Over the summer at Camp Shriver, she was asked to take part in a photo shoot for Special Olympics New Jersey's new website. Little did I know that she would become one of four featured athletes on the website and have her picture plastered all over! Is she one of their best athletes? No. But everyone loves Delaney, and Delaney loves everyone at Special Olympics. Delaney feels at home there. She can go work out at the gym there and always see a friend she knows. Delaney has a place she belongs.

Because of Delaney and because she has Williams syndrome, I have found a place to help not only her but also others with developmental disabilities. With our local YMCA, I now volunteer as the Special

Olympics New Jersey Coordinator, bringing Special Olympics to our town and helping to develop positive peer relationships and a healthy outlook for Delaney. There is now another girl her age with Williams syndrome on our track team. I love watching them together. They have this incredible bond whenever they see each other. You always hope that your daughter will find that in a friend.

Delaney is an amazing person who requires much dedication from us as her parents, but she loves everyone and everyone loves her. Everyone is always happy to see her walk into a room. She has changed our lives forever and in a wonderful way by opening our eyes to a whole new world and new experiences. Who knew this is where our princess would take us over the last eleven years? We are so grateful to have her as our daughter.

Picture Credit: Copyright © 2013 Heather O'Connell Photography

Chapter 4

Joys and Victories

One of the great dichotomies of Williams syndrome is that, when we get the diagnosis, many of us can't imagine ever feeling joy about it; and yet, a year or two down the road, we look back and are awestruck that we ever felt any kind of grief about what has become a source of unrelenting joy. It is no coincidence that this chapter, "Joys and Victories," is the longest in the book.

Hey, Bud
Adam Kimball

Adam Kimball is the father of three children—Makena, 13; Addysen, 10; and Asher, 8. He lives in Roswell, Georgia, with his best friend and wife of sixteen years, Janelle. While he spends entirely too much time throughout the week pretending he's important—as a VP for a large global service organization—he truly loves to travel, read, make his wife laugh, convince his daughters to call him "your majesty," and sing Elvis's songs now and again. Most of all, Adam loves to be Dad and is passionately pursuing not messing up his kids too much each day.

Just like you, perhaps I could never have imagined the utter heartbreak that resulted out of an event so highly anticipated as the birth of my son. It was like riding a roller coaster that I couldn't wait to ride for the first time. But, as I reached the top, it stopped. That's where I'd arrived: Williams syndrome. Today, however, probably also like many of you, I now recognize that WS wasn't just a destination I had arrived at and now simply have to suffer through. Rather, it is the unveiling of a whole new perspective on life.

Asher Kent Kimball is the single greatest thing to ever happen to me. Hands down. End of discussion. No disrespect intended to my marvelous, and quite frankly, saint-like best friend and wife, Janelle, nor toward my two amazingly brilliant little ladies, Makena and Addysen (as without them Asher's lessons may have been lost on me anyway). He is simply because he's taught me what truly living is. As a result of Asher, my life is … well … full. There's deeper laughter, greater sadness, and stomach-wrenching frustration, and there is an overwhelming feeling of passion in so much more of everyday life. I appreciate the experience of these intense emotions through a storyboard of moments like I   never even knew I could.

Over the past eight years since Asher was born, amidst the innumerable times my wife and I have been at the precipice of "crazy," that little boy shows us what life is truly about. He let us in on this incredible, but elusive, secret. Something the majority of the world is missing out on—appreciating each and every moment no matter how simple, and to just allow each experience, good or bad, to soak into your soul—and simply smile.

One of those moments came not too long ago. After over seven years, among many other things, Asher still didn't speak. We knew him, so we knew what he wanted based on the grunt or the pointing or the signing. Up until he was six years old, we had held out hope that he may someday clearly ask for a drink of water or say "I love you" to us. However, we had to move on; and so, we had resigned ourselves to the reality that he would never speak. We had accepted it, were okay with it—and we were moving on. Then "it" happened. And in the same way he's taught me to appreciate the simplicity of life in so many other ways, he continued that lesson.

Now, when I say "simple," I don't want to belittle any of this. Yes, I believe simple is the point—an appreciation of the simplest of moments we encounter every day. It doesn't mean there's a lack of depth or complexity within each of those moments. I dare say it's quite the opposite, in fact. Simple is basic, raw, and real.

Simple means you can't *do* anything to make it better. Simple just is. Ultimately, that's the real victory in this—thriving on the simple moments.

For me, one of those moments came in October 2012 as I entered the house and heard my boy shuffle up the hallway. Asher saw me, raised one hand above his head in a careless "How's it going" kind of wave, and called out, "Hey, Bud!" As my mental process tried to catch up with my ears and my mouth dropped open in shock at this overwhelming instance, Asher gave me a sideways glance like, *I knew you'd like that*, and he continued on his way.

After a few more months, his vocabulary quickly expanded, and he's become quite the little motor mouth. Certainly his speech is far from perfect, but to my wife and me, it's the clearest voice in our world. Asher is talking—and every time I hear him say, "I love you" or

"Night, Daddy" as he heads to bed, I can't help but feel like I'm watching something so pure and good, that nothing could be better. That is simple, and I love that I can just absorb that moment in a way I couldn't with my other two children as they began speaking all those years ago.

So as a parent of a child with WS, don't let anyone, or more importantly yourself, ever feel sorry for you. Now I'm sure, that just like myself, you appreciate those sincere attempts by friends and family to recognize that this whole "special needs" thing is the toughest road you've walked, or that the depth of the pain and frustration can understandably overwhelm us at times. In those moments, we can't help but wonder "what if" our kiddos were "normal"? Then, we would be leading the same tired old story so many others in our world are—which, admittedly, can be appealing during the tough moments … but at the expense of losing the richness of all the other moments that our eyes are forever opened to? No way.

While there is, and will always be, a level of mourning when I think of all the "typical" things that will be different, or not available, for Asher, I am quickly reminded that I've seen the purpose of this. I am immeasurably blessed beyond anything I deserve, and I recognize it because of Asher. I've been given a window to view the world through which even the smallest of blessings is magnified to a degree that makes "normal" simply boring. All you need to do is watch them. Watch the wonder of their beautiful minds as they observe whatever they are focused on at that moment. Watch how that beautiful person can light up a room, change a school, and re-architect the foundations of your family. Watch how their unabashed forwardness opens doors to relationships and conversations and opportunities that would otherwise never have been available to you.

So I actually, and truly, feel a bit sorry for people who don't have an Asher. They haven't been let in on this marvelous secret. How crazy that this little genetic deletion, a piece of biological life missing, would actually serve to fill in the gaps in our own lives. Celebrate it! Let it knock you to your knees and change your life, if it hasn't already. Just like the first time you hear, "Hey, Bud."

Bethany's Standing Ovation

Barbara Zinka

Barbara Zinka lives in Derry, New Hampshire, with her husband, Mike, and youngest daughter, Bethany, who has Williams syndrome. They also have three older daughters. Barbara enjoys photography and scrapbooking as well as camping in Wells, Maine.

We live in the town of Derry, New Hampshire, which has two middle schools for grades six through eight. Each school has approximately 300 students per grade, and each grade is divided into three teams. Each middle school holds three promotion activities toward the end of the school year for the teams.

I drive a special education wheelchair bus, and while my daughter, Bethany, was in middle school, I was allowed to pick her up in the afternoon prior to making my high school run. A brother and sister whom I transported at the time required a nurse on the bus for medical reasons. The brother's nurse, JC, rode with me each morning and afternoon. Not only did the nurse and I become friends; she also developed a strong bond with Bethany due to her outgoing personality.

The first promotion activity was a trip to an amusement park, Canobie Lake Park, about twenty minutes away, and I received a form from school to be a volunteer chaperone. Knowing Bethany's reservations to try any new activities without a lot of prompting and encouragement, I decided to go. JC's student happened to have appointments the day of the field trip, so she had the day off and asked if she could join us, to which I gladly agreed. Throughout the day, it warmed my heart to see how many of the students cheerfully greeted Bethany and stopped to ask about her favorite rides. Bethany rode all of the thrill rides, including the Extreme Frisbee and the wooden roller coaster, as well as some of the more sedate rides. She probably wouldn't have ridden any of the

81

thrill rides without my prodding and encouragement. The highlight of Bethany's day was having fried dough and pizza!

The second activity, the promotion dance, was held the Friday preceding the promotion ceremony. A Hummer limousine took small groups of students from the front of the school to the back, where the cafeteria was decorated in a tropical theme. On the walk from our car to where the other students were waiting, students kept calling Bethany's name and commenting about how beautiful she looked. Her response was, "I know." I kept trying to get her to say, "Thank you," but she knew that she looked beautiful. As the limousine carrying her and two of her friends drove off, I quickly ran around the other side of the school to the back so that I could take pictures of her getting out of the limo. She acted like a rock star, waving to teachers and advisors as she was getting out of the limo and walking into the school.

I was given special permission by the school administration to stay at the dance to supervise Bethany because we were all a bit concerned about how she would react to the loud music. As I was trying to inconspicuously stand along the wall, she came over to me and said, "Mom, you can go now. I'm having fun." I didn't know whether to laugh or cry! I did a little of both. Shortly afterward, I could see her bopping around the dance floor, making sure that she danced with every single person there. As I got ready to leave, her case coordinator told me that she would watch out for her and call me when Bethany was ready to leave. Even though the dance lasted until 10:00 p.m., Bethany called at about 9:20 p.m. saying that she had had enough. As we were driving home, Bethany told me, "This was the best night of my life!"

About two weeks before the promotion ceremony, a secretary at Bethany's middle school called to say that Bethany would be given an award and a fifty-dollar savings bond during the promotion ceremony. She wouldn't tell me anything else. I tried to keep it a secret from the rest of the family so that Bethany wouldn't catch on. Bethany's team leader e-mailed me a few days before the ceremony saying that eight awards would be given during the ceremony and that Bethany's would be the third or fourth one given out.

The promotion ceremony was held in the high school gymnasium because it has enough room for all of the students' family and friends.

Two of Bethany's sisters, my husband, my mother, JC, and I sat in the second row of the chair seating, directly behind Bethany's team. Each of the eighth-grade teams had picked out a song to play as the team entered the gym. Team 8-1, Bethany's team, was the first to enter. We all anxiously watched as more than ninety students entered the gym. With the last name Zinka, Bethany was at the end of the group. She could be seen bopping along and waving to people all through the audience as the team was making its way to the seats. We couldn't help but smile and laugh.

The other two teams made their way into the gym. After the students were all settled, we heard the usual speeches. The eighth-grade chorus went to a set of risers to sing a few songs, and as Bethany was making her way to the front, she again waved to other students as she passed. Two fellow students assisted her on her way to the top riser. While the chorus was singing, Bethany was joining in and rocking away. When the songs were completed, she made her way back to her seat, once again waving to the audience as well as fellow students.

We patiently listened to the keynote speaker. Then, it was time for the awards. I told the family about her award a few days before the ceremony and had sworn them all to secrecy. The first three awards were given out, and the audience clapped for each student. Extra cheers came from different spots in the gym from families and friends of the students receiving the awards. The teacher giving out the fourth award started talking about how the next student puts a smile on so many faces each day and that she would be greatly missed at Gilbert H. Hood Middle School. She then said, "The Award in Courage goes to Bethany Zinka." Our family began clapping when, suddenly, the entire gymnasium stood up to give Bethany a standing ovation. I felt the tears fill my eyes as I looked around at the entire bleacher section on three sides as well as the portable chairs. The boisterous cheers continued on until Bethany was seated back in her chair. Three more awards were given out and the audience applauded for each student, but there were no more standing ovations.

We listened to another speech before it was time to award the diplomas. Bethany's team was the first to be called. As each student's name was called, people clapped and the friends and families of the students could be heard cheering more loudly than the rest of the audience. Ninety-something names were called before hers. When the announcer called her name, the entire eighth grade stood up and enthusiastically cheered for her. Before we knew it, everyone in the entire gymnasium was once again on their feet, giving her a standing ovation. Our family and JC were all in tears. Bethany, as though she were a rock star, waved her hands to everyone as she walked back to her seat, and the cheering continued the whole way.

Tooth Fairy's Mistaken Identity

Dannette Cates

Dannette Cates is the mother of three children, Jacob, Dakota, and Jordan. Dannette lives in Salem, Wisconsin, with her husband, Joseph, and their children, where she loves gardening, reading, and spending time with her family. Dannette works as a special education paraprofessional and a Family Engagement Cocoordinator for three counties in southeast Wisconsin.

It was a sunny, spring day, a great day for a drive to the children's hospital for a doctor's appointment for my daughter, Dakota, who has Williams syndrome. Dakota and I were making plans for her tenth birthday party, which was only two weeks away. She wanted a princess theme complete with a princess cake.

We talked about what she wanted to do when she grew up. She explained that she would like a job as Cinderella at Disney World and that when she was not working, she would just live in the castle with her friend, Kristen. Dakota was, after all, a girl whom we called Princess at home.

"Mom, I have a secret," Dakota said. "Is it okay to tell you the secret?"

I nervously answered, "Yes, because the rule is all kids need to tell their moms all secrets."

Dakota seemed a bit hesitant but asked, "Mom, are you the tooth fairy?"

I hesitated. I was surprised by the question, but I was quite proud that Dakota had figured this out on her own. *What great cognitive thinking for a girl who "lives" in a fairy tale,* I thought. I was very happy that she had figured it out at about the same time that other children her age would have.

"Yes, I am the tooth fairy," I responded.

Dakota looked quite impressed and excited as she inquired, "So, Mom, when you go to all the people's houses, do you fly or do you drive?"

I laughed so hard that I had to maneuver the car back onto the road. I explained to Dakota that I was only *her* tooth fairy and that all the other kids' moms were their tooth fairies. I did mention that as much

as I would like to be able to fly, I don't. I told her that I would simply sneak into her room when she was sleeping and slip the tooth out from under her pillow.

It was the best compliment I have ever received!

When Dakota was in the first grade, she asked if she was a "real" princess. Her dad and I would respond, "Yes, you are a real princess." She continued to ask because some of her classmates said that she wasn't a real princess.

I often volunteered in her first-grade classroom. As I sat down to read a book to the class, a little girl raised her hand and excitedly asked, "Mrs. Dakota's mom, Dakota says she is a real princess and we want to know if this is true." All the other little girls in the story circle anxiously awaited my answer.

Without thinking, I said, "Well, I am the queen of the Cates house. So, yes, that would make Dakota a real princess." The girls in the room looked at Dakota and me with awe and admiration. Dakota was a true princess.

Now, Dakota is twenty-one, and we still call her Princess. After all, we consider ourselves royalty to have such a regal gift from God. Sometimes Dakota still lives in her fairy tale world, which reminds us not to take life too seriously.

This destination that Williams syndrome has led us to has enhanced our lives. Our journey has given us compassion, patience, and understanding that we may not have otherwise experienced. We have met many other amazing individuals with Williams syndrome, and their families have touched our lives. We consider them our extended family. We have found that parents of children with Williams syndrome are a great resource. We have shared triumphs, struggles, joys, and sometimes tears with them. They have given us strength, advice, and friendship.

Having a child with Williams syndrome has shaped our lives in so many new and different directions. It has given our two sons empathy and patience that will benefit them throughout their lives. It has strengthened our marriage and our family bond, encouraging us to truly work as a team.

A friend once asked, "If you could magically change Dakota's Williams syndrome, would you?" I selfishly said, "No." I could not give up the enrichment it has brought to our lives, our newfound Williams syndrome family, and our "real" princess.

Stinky Face

Erin Putman

Erin Putman resides in New Jersey with her husband, Todd, and son, Evan. She is a special ed teacher who loves to sing, read, and blog at www.musingsbymama.com.

Evan is our amazing son. He was diagnosed with Williams syndrome just after his first birthday. We were blindsided, not expecting the diagnosis at all. Since then, we have learned all we can about the syndrome, have made many new friends across the country (and the world), and have come to accept our new reality.

Starting at about fifteen months of age, Evan began early intervention therapies. He receives speech, occupational, and physical therapy, as well as hippotherapy, which is occupational therapy on horseback. He has progressed from barely eating purees and a few ounces of PediaSure at a time to eating grilled cheese sandwiches, PBJ, and other foods. He is also doing well with his speech and language and recently has really been on a language "boom," as his therapist likes to call it. Here is a little story of one of the first times I heard him say a word that I had longed to hear since before he was even born.

One chilly Sunday in early 2013, Evan was curled up in his weighted blanket and our reversible Steelers/Eagles cover. He lay against my chest and listened to me read to him. He had been fighting a really rough cold, and we were on day four of this whopper of an illness. The poor thing was so weak, and he could only keep down liquids. His body was working so hard to fight off the germs that were taking over his little system. A moat of towels surrounded us because he sometimes would vomit from the combination of congestion and reflux.

But Mama, but Mama, what if I were a swamp creature with slimy, smelly seaweed hanging from my body?

Then I would live by the swamp and take care of you always. I'd tell you, "I love you, my slimy swamp monster."

Evan weakly tried to flip pages for a few seconds and then gave up and just listened to me read. At that time, he had been doing little *mmm* noises in response to repetitive text and also when singing songs that repeated. Sometimes he sounded like he was trying to say either the letter or the word, but rarely was it clear or accurate.

But Mama, but Mama, what if I were a super smelly skunk and I smelled so bad that my name was Stinky Face?

Then I'd plunk you in a bubble bath! But if you still smelled stinky, I wouldn't mind. I'd whisper in your ear, "I love you, Stinky Face."

I then heard a little voice say, "Ma-ma …" and it was coming from the ball of blankets and towels in my lap.

"Ma-ma …" he repeated.

"Mama?" I whispered, but it was more like a gasp.

Evan looked up at me, and over-enunciated like he thought I didn't hear him correctly, "*Ma … Ma.*"

My eyes stung immediately with hot tears, and I squeezed him tightly. We went back and forth saying "mama" to each other for a few minutes, and Todd joined in from the recliner.

I realized in that moment that Evan had been listening to me for months while I read him the same story, the one with the alligator with big teeth that he likes to touch and kiss, the one where we repeat the word *mama* over and over every few pages. The times prior to this moment when he crawled to me saying "mamamamamamamamaamama" and crying had been sound play—his way of telling me he needed help.

But this was the word *Mama*. And I knew in that moment that one day he would come toddling over to me and say it to address me. And sure enough, he has.

In an amazing way, chromosomes can both matter immensely and mean nothing in moments like this. The moment of hearing Evan say "Mama" feels like a victory in our house.

At the same time, in that moment, when the tears stung and my heart swelled, not one deletion, syndrome, or special need was present in my mind.

Just pure love.

(The book quoted is *I Love You, Stinky Face* by Lisa McCourt.)

Do You Believe in Magic?
Erin Rupolo

Erin Rupolo has two children, Barrett and Sophie. She lives in Maryland and loves helping others, meeting new people, and spending time with her friends and family.

There is something magical about Sophie. I remember that when we first got our diagnosis and Sophie was only three months old, I kept reading one common theme about having a child with Williams syndrome, and that was the joy that they bring to their families and the people who know them. At the time, Sophie was a colicky nightmare, and the word *joy* was the last one I would have used to refer to her … but, boy, have times changed! Sophie made us wait until she was six months old to shine her first smile, and not a day has gone by that she has not shared that beautiful, big smile with the world. It's amazing—she doesn't even have to say a word, and still people from all over gravitate to her. It's as if she radiates some form of energy that people can feel. When she was younger, it used to creep me out, but over the last four years, I have come to accept it, embrace it, and enjoy it!

Sophie is a friendly, smiley, sassy little girl with a huge personality. Everyone who works at our local grocery store would have to agree. They all know Sophie by name and look forward to our Monday morning shopping trips. She is always quick to be sure everyone is greeted with a friendly smile, a hello, and finally a "What's your name?" Afterward, she will repeat their names and end with a "Nice to meet you!" It gets people every time! To see this little, cute four-year-old with such polite, friendly manners—who wouldn't want to eat her up?

Ever since Sophie was an infant, she has had a dash of sass added to her endearing personality, whether it was her refusal to drink her bottle as a baby—with closed eyes and her head turned the other way, a downright protest while being tested followed by her telling the tester that her earrings were "just beautiful"; calling out, "Mommeeeey, Mommeeeey, ERIN!" in order to get my attention; or telling me, "Just a minute. I'm busy," when I need her to attend to something, Sophie has always known what she wants, when she wants it, and—surprisingly—exactly how to get it. She has a way about her sassiness that makes you want to smile. Even though she is stubborn like her mommy and daddy, she is absolutely a people pleaser!

On the first day she was picked up by the bus to attend preschool, she was named the "mayor of the bus." She climbs up those big stairs and makes her morning announcement of "Hi, friends!" She is the first to tell you that you "look beautiful" or that you are "soooo cute," and her timing is always perfect! Her teachers describe her as "very social and happy in school," saying, "She loves to greet people and is very caring toward others. She will comfort, praise and correct other children verbally. She is a natural leader who likes to let her peers know what we are doing and when they need to 'Sit down!' or 'Be quiet.'"

At home, she is a character too. She loves to ruffle her brother's feathers by reciting things she has heard directly out of his mouth, such as, "Nana nana boo boo. I have your car," as well as offering him support when he is sad. Just this morning, her brother was upset and crying; Sophie put her arms around him and told him, "It will be okay. I am here." She also loves to warm my heart too! Every night I get my nightly after-bath hugs, and just the other night she leaned in to give me a hug, pat my back, and say, "Mommy, you best of my friend."

She just has a way of making everyone feel so special! When she receives a gift, she is always overdramatic about how much she loves it and how thankful she is. It doesn't matter if it's a picture, an article of clothing, or, her favorite, a baby doll. Sophie just has a knack for making you feel important and special all at the same time. What amazes me the most is that she doesn't have to even say a word, and people around her can instantly see this magic she radiates.

The magic that Sophie has brought into my life is indescribable. She is truly amazing, and I am so grateful to have her as a part of our family! She is now a beautiful four-year-old who is happy, smart, sassy, and the most endearing little person you could ever imagine. I reflect back now to those dark days after we had just learned of Sophie's diagnosis.

It makes me chuckle that I actually thought she may never smile or that my life had changed for the worse. Sophie continues to teach me and those around her what living is all about, and I thank her every day for adding such enchanted beauty to my life!

A Blessing
Kelly Connell

Kelly Connell lives in Boston, Massachusetts, and has been teaching for fifteen years. She is the happiest when she is travelling the world.

I can't believe it has been almost ten years since my first niece was born. I knew from the moment of Emerson's birth that I would never be able to say no to her. This explains why I found myself outside, behind fifty people in line at Chuck E. Cheese, in the dark, cold rain.

Emerson was 364 days old when the test results came back. My sister, Amy, was devastated. Growing up, I remember that Amy always dreamed of having her own kids. Amy is a very determined person. When she has her mind set on an idea and life does not unfold accordingly, it rocks her world. Amy's idealized version of Emerson's adolescence was well orchestrated almost from conception. Emerson would have my sister's red hair, be a bit shy, and keep all her dolls organized in rows. Never in this time had she imagined Emerson would be diagnosed with Williams syndrome.

This was a hard pill to swallow. From the start, Emerson did not sleep at night, she did not nap, and she spit up everything she ate. The milk hurt her stomach, and the simple act of peeing caused her terrible discomfort. It was a long, sleepless, and stressful period of time for

Amy and her husband. In addition to witnessing their daughter's pain, they were grappling with their own emotions. Accepting that their daughter may not go off to college or live an independent life was heartbreaking. "Will I ever be able to meet my daughter for coffee?" is a question my sister still battles with today.

It was a dark period for me as well. I felt helpless and frustrated that I could not ease Amy's suffering. When you see someone you love go through this, you want to take away all the pain. But I could not, and that was the hardest part.

I am very lucky to be so involved in Emerson's life. I have seen her reach many milestones, taken her on vacations, and enjoyed going with her to the Williams syndrome kids' camp each summer. Emerson is independent and strong willed. It is impossible to ignore her presence. She can walk into a room and light it up with her energy and enthusiasm. I have also had the opportunity to work at the Williams syndrome adult camps and have made many wonderful friends. When people with WS get together, it is like nothing I have ever seen before. The camp radiates a collective aura that is a great source of happiness for all involved. I was once asked a simple, yet complex, question by a documentarian making a movie: "What is Williams syndrome?" My response, after a long, dead silence was, "Williams syndrome is both a blessing and a curse." The physical challenge and stigmas that accompany those with special needs will always be a struggle, but it is the blessings that Emerson brings that amaze me.

We all live busy lives and, therefore, can so easily overlook the important things. Emerson is not wired like this and never has been. When your child gets a diagnosis like Williams syndrome, you find yourself caught up in fears about the future. Will she be successful in school? Can she live on her own? With all this worry, we forget one of the most important life lessons—to be present. Emerson never forgets to be present. She focuses on the people she experiences, not the situation, and there are a lot of good lessons in that. In her world, every day is an opportunity to discover joy, even in the most unexpected places.

So there we were, finally inside Chuck E. Cheese—after roughly forty minutes of rain-soaked line standing. To my great dismay, the token machine was broken, and there was yet another line to tackle. I had pretty much reached my limit and decided to forge on with no game tokens. Anyone who has had the pleasure of spending time in one of these establishments would cast her doubt on this decision. Emerson did not skip a beat. She grabbed my hand with a big smile, and we embraced each game with a quick glance or a smack here and there. For over an hour we bounced through the crowd, engaging everyone with a positive word or high five. Em recovered a couple of loose basketballs and dribbled in circles. We spent a bit of time on the merry-go-round (on someone else's dime), and with one lone token found on the floor, we played her beloved Bop-It game. She mounted a horse and, even without motion, cried "Kiki, look at me go!" Last, a rocket-ship popsicle was the cherry on the sundae for my Em. As we walked out the door, she looked up at me and said, "I love Chuck E. Cheese Boston, and I love you."

Through Emerson's eyes, I get a moment of clarity and peace. I am able to slow down and take each moment as it comes. Her ability to make me stop and question the way I perceive life is the greatest blessing I have been given, even if it takes a night at Chuck E. Cheese to be reminded of this.

Best Day Ever
Tess Roach

Tess Roach lives in Cove, Texas, with her husband and two daughters, Ana, 7, and Addyson, 5. She is a freelance editor who enjoys playing board games, snuggling on the couch, and generally spending time with her family.

When I hear other people's stories about their experiences with Williams syndrome, I find there is usually a shudder effect. Perhaps a family had to take their one-month-old baby in for heart surgery or deal with severe bullying in middle school. Those are truly harrowing tales. For us—at least so far—our story hasn't induced any shuddering.

Certainly, the day we got the diagnosis when Addyson was eighteen months old was a turning point, and it took us a while to wrap our minds around what our lives would look like from that point forward, but we haven't had any of the really negative or scary experiences that many people have, thank goodness. In her five years, Addyson hasn't needed heart or kidney surgery or any medical procedure more significant than an ultrasound and an EKG, and our biggest concern right now is monitoring her blood pressure and getting her to eat enough. I know the serious stuff could still be down the road, but right now, she is just a bundle of fun.

In our family, Addyson is known for bringing the sunshine to any day, but she doesn't always do it in the same way. Sometimes it's through her sheer love of life, her uninhibited savoring of the joy in every day and animated expressions of her feelings. On a plain, stay-at-home day when we're doing nothing more than cleaning the house, she'll announce that it's the "best day ever" and ask when we're going to space on a rocket ship. (We keep saying, "Someday," and "We gotta get a rocket ship first!") Other times, Addyson spices up our lives with her sassiness. One day, she quoted *Wreck-It Ralph* in a way I'd rather she hadn't. Out of the blue, when I hadn't said *anything,* she asked, "Mom, why are you so freakin' annoying?" It's hard to chastise her when I'm laughing and her older sister, Ana, is howling.

From times when our families have gotten together, her older cousins have racked up a list of "Addyisms" that crack them up. Sheridan, for example, experienced the way Addyson gives compliments so freely when Addyson announced, "Sheridan, I like your nose." Melissa remembers one of her nonsensical comments, when she said, "Look, Melissa! I don't see a rainbow!" And then Addyson displayed her humility as we were leaving Aunt Susan's house one day, saying, "You can cry now. I'm leaving."

When she was younger, around three, she would rant, but the rants were *hilarious.* If I got onto her about something, she would yell, "Mama! Don't say dat. Again! Never. Every DAY!" When Aunt Jeannie witnessed these rants, she would have to turn and leave the room to avoid laughing out loud and drawing my ire as I tried with all my might to stay serious and address the disrespect issue.

In school, Addyson continues her shenanigans. She appears to be the most popular kid in her school, which is limited to preschool and kindergarten. Every time I'm there with her, it takes us forever to walk down the hall because all the teachers and aides stop to talk to her (*her,* not me). But she doesn't spare them the sass. Her teacher told me that one day during snack time, when everyone was happily eating and nothing was amiss, Addyson looked her in the eye and said, "You don't scare me at all." Thank goodness the teacher laughed, but I thought, *That may be funny now, but it won't be so funny if she tries it when she's fourteen!*

Of course, some of her funniest moments have been embarrassing as well—not terribly embarrassing, but enough. We were at Disney World and got on a bus at our hotel to go to the park. It was already a bit crowded, so my husband and Ana sat a few rows behind Addyson and me. When more people got on at the next stop, I pulled Addyson up into my lap to free up the seat next to me. A nine-year-old girl sat next to us, and we struck up a conversation. Addyson, naturally, talked to her quite a bit, and we found out her name, where she lived, what grade she was in, what her favorite ride was—all that important stuff.

Then, at a lull in the conversation, Addyson turned around and *very loudly* said, "Hey, Daddy! We got a girl!" A perplexed smile came across the girl's face as I shook my head and laughed, trying to get it together before I could offer some kind of explanation and reassurance that we did not intend to kidnap her.

The moments I love the most are those when Addyson's ever-present optimism comes out, even when she may not intend it. That happened one day when she climbed into the car after school, complaining that a little boy had called her dumb. Ever the big sister, Ana said, "Did you tell him, 'I'm not dumb. Don't call me dumb'?" Addyson replied sadly, "No." Ana said, "Addyson, you have to be brave! And courageous!" After just a moment of thought, Addyson smirked and responded, "I'm gonna be gorgeous." I concurred that hers was a pretty good revenge.

Most of my experiences with Addyson are flat-out fun. She surprises me with her wit and her genuine joy on a daily basis. Her love for life is a constant reminder to me that I need to look for the good in every day—why *can't* a stay-at-home cleaning day be a great day? It can! Finding limitless joy in the simple things has to be Addyson's most significant gift at this point. If we let that girl go swimming with Ana and her cousins, eat Grandmother's bacon, and have snow cones all in one day, I'm pretty sure her happy meter would break. Best. Day. Ever.

Hwhees, Squeals, and Missions ~~(Im)~~Possible
Todd Putman

Todd Putman is the husband of Erin and father of two-and-a-half-year-old Evan, who has Williams syndrome. He lives in New Jersey, just outside of Philadelphia. He enjoys nature afoot or in a kayak, photography, live music, watching a variety of sports, and home brewing bold ales and lagers.

As a parent of a child with Williams syndrome, I think there is a temptation, at times, for me to think of my relationship with Evan as being different than those between my friends and their "typically developing" kids. While they share stories about walking and talking at typical ages, we're offering tales of the otherwise remedial things Evan does while dreaming of him doing the things their kids do. The harm in that sort of results-based relationship is that when I focus beyond today, I miss out on the joy of Evan's now. It's not Evan vis-à-vis the rest of the world. It's Evan, amazing member of the world, starring in the lead male role of my life. So, with that in mind, I'd like to share some of my favorite Evan moments, which help to define his unique beauty.

But first, some context.

To know our family—not the polite, domesticated, dare I say, aristocratic version you see at church on Sunday mornings, but the real

us—is to know silliness and love. Sure, we'll all ivory-handled canes and polished monocles in those public settings, but in our natural environment, you're more likely to see us decked out in our best pajama pants, comfy T-shirts, and slippers. In

100

such situations, absent the constant threat of public humiliation, we're known to produce goofy sounds, make the kinds of faces our parents told us would "stick like that" (liars!), and laugh until it hurts. That's just our way.

When Evan was around thirteen months old, he and I were playing on the floor. While the exact specifics are hazy, I'm sure whatever we were doing was interrupted ad nauseam by his pressing a button on a toy to produce flashing lights and hypnotic music. Clearly, that was before our eighteen-month visit to Dr. Mervis, after which 95 percent of those toys were quarantined in a far corner of our unfinished basement where the cricket spiders dwell—but I digress.

Whatever we were doing that day inspired me to give a few big shouts of "Weeeeeeee!" In his pre-twelve-month days, that sort of outburst might have drawn a curious glance from the lad, but thirteen-month-old Evan, being fully aware that his dada is a loon, kept playing intently. Soon thereafter, he repeated whatever action it was that inspired my "Weeeeeeee!" I responded in kind with another "Weeeeeeee!" The difference this time was that Evan looked me right in the eyes, and in a tiny, raspy voice, very deliberately said, "Hwhee." Knowing that his dad is a numbers guru who believes strongly in the concepts of outliers and the necessity of a good random sample, Evan repeated "hwhee" at least five times. It was his first repeated "word." It was no mistake. It was awesome.

Evan said "hwhee" several dozen times afterward, but it has seemingly worked its way out of his lexicon. Today, our conversations take on the following tone:

> Evan: Eh.
>
> Daddy: Eh.
>
> Evan: Eeeee!
>
> Daddy: Eeeee!
>
> Evan: (with lungs at full capacity and veins on his tiny, porcelain neck first rising and then bulging as he crescendos) Ahhhhhhhhhheeeeeeeeeeeeeeeeeeee!*

The audible portion of this squeal-like sound of delight starts off like the opening sequence of The Flintstones *when Fred's boss pulls the string attached to the bird's tail that signals "quittin' time" and then slides up an octave to sound like a cop car peeling out after an escaped convict. It then finishes, or so our dog, Zoey, tells me, at a pitch rivaled only by the finest dog whistles.*

Daddy: (attempts to make the sound Evan just made, injures his throat, and then says) Eh.

Evan: Eeeeee!

While part of me longs for a day when he and I will converse at length about important things like what his favorite line from *Yo Gabba Gabba* is, I enjoy the Evan moments of today with equal delight. (Coincidentally, I intend to raise my son to give the correct answer: "It's when Brobee says, 'I forgot, I'm still *hungry*!' and reaches for his sandwich, which has fallen on the ground, just before the Tiny Ugly Germs make their debut.") In the absence of such philosophical discourse, I can only reflect upon my favorite Evan moments.

At about seventeen months, Evan had mastered every mode of locomotion except walking, moon-walking, skipping, hopscotch, and the worm. So I should have seen it coming. Next to our entertainment center is a desktop computer I had hooked up after we cut the cable cord so that we could watch streaming video online. One of Evan's favorite things to do is open and close doors. It took about thirty seconds of that desktop being hooked up for Evan to rip off the HD-DVD drawer cover (yes, I was *the* guy who picked HD-DVD over Blu-Ray in 2007). In a desperate effort to save the helpless CD-RW drawer cover, we placed his Laugh & Learn: Musical Learning Chair in front of the computer. While I don't know for certain, my best guess is that Evan somehow saw that scene from *Mission: Impossible* where Tom Cruise's character was lowered from the ceiling of a CIA stronghold through a series of laser beams and extracted data from a computer while suspended in midair. That is my working theory as that is the only thing I can think of that is as complex as what Evan did that day.

First, he made sure he was dressed for the occasion—his best orange Skidder socks (for extra grip), red-and-black-striped onesie, and mismatched blue baseball pants—a clear one-up over Tom Cruise in all black. Seeing his book on top of the entertainment center, Evan moved to the side with the toy chair and crawled atop it. Next, he deftly scaled the computer. For a brief moment, realizing he was at a theretofore uncharted two-foot precipice, he wobbled. Undeterred, he steadied himself and lunged for the book, several feet away. He did it! Mission *Possible*! Needless to say, I picked my jaw up off the floor and helped him down. His reward: I read him the story he had worked so hard to reach.

When all is said and done and I am swapping stories with my friends, I take immense pride in Evan. Just like their kids, he had (or will have) a first word, a first crawl, and a first whatever the flavor of the month is for other proud papas; but the goal is not to be like others. The goal is to make semi-audible sounds of delight, sounds that are amplifications of the joys of my heart. The goal is to find unmatched joy in the exploration of new places beyond where any of us have been before or could even imagine going. The world is immense and its forces powerful. We are small and helpless. But in the small places and quiet, singular moments, my pride in my son—no, our pride in our sons and daughters—grows big.

Evan is missing twenty-some genes. He has tens of thousands. We are all snowflakes and, like them, our time is fleeting. Rather than wish they would melt away to make our commute easier or try to scoop them up quickly and put them in our freezer to save them from their fate, why not bask in their beauty and let the temporary limitations of days without words or steps be invitations to the complexities of the wonderment of the gifts of life, love, and the possible not yet achieved?

Hello, New Day
Vena A. Glendon

Vena Glendon lives in New Jersey with her husband, Peter. Together they have seven children. She loves writing, baking, and spending as much time as she can with her eighteen grandchildren, who live in several different states throughout the country.

This story is about a very special little boy, my three-year-old grandson Godric. I am sure that every grandparent will tell you that they love each of their grandchildren "the same." I certainly agree this is true; however, I believe that we love each of them in very different ways.

Before Godric was born, I was experiencing one of the lowest times of my life. When your heart aches, you tend to forget about all the positive things you have and only feel the pain. I was lucky enough to have a son and daughter-in-law who must have seen how I was feeling. They gave me the one gift that would change my life forever. They allowed me the honor of being in the delivery room when their beautiful son was born. From the moment this precious child came into the world and took his first breath, there was a bond that was so immediate and strong, I knew it would be forever.

Godric was tiny, weighing just a little over five pounds, but he was perfect in every other way. It was not until he was about eighteen months old that he was diagnosed with Williams syndrome.

My son and his wife also have three other children, so as you can imagine, life can get quite hectic for them with four children in the family. Therefore, my husband and I are always more than willing to help out by bringing Godric home to spend time with us. I believe this is good for him, and I know it is wonderful for the two of us.

Godric has taught me just how precious life is and that I should be thankful for each day that I am able to share with him. It is because of this lesson that I feel it is my responsibility to help him learn what a gift life is and to always look forward to each new day for what it has to offer.

Ever since he was an infant, whenever he spent time with us, we would begin each morning the same way. I would carry him to the front door, open it, and say "Hello, new day," and we would wave to the new day before us. Now every morning when he wakes up in our home, he is always ready for our special ritual. Godric loves doing this so much that we have even started including the sentence, "I'm very happy to see you." We have been doing this for over three years now. It still amazes me how happy this makes both of us. In fact, you might be surprised at how

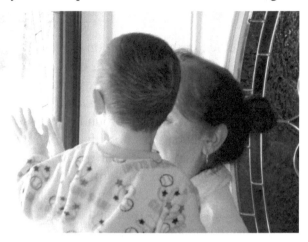

this little ritual with the very big meaning has actually caught on with everyone in our home. Godric is always excited to do this, and anyone who is within earshot—whether it's my husband, my twenty-year-old granddaughter, Godric's siblings, or anyone else who happens to be visiting—can't help but be drawn into our special hello to the new day. It really made me chuckle the first time our granddaughter's twenty-two-year-old boyfriend came to the front door with us and waved to the "new day." Now that Godric has a baby sister, I am sure we will include her in our morning ritual too.

Over the past three years, through the articles I have read and the research I have done, I have come to believe that one of the most important and certainly one of the most comforting things for a child with Williams syndrome is consistency. We will continue going to the front door each morning and taking the time to say hello to the new day for as long as Godric is willing to do it.

I know the day may come when he may feel he's "too big" or "too grown up" to do something so silly. Of course, this will break my heart just a little, but until then I will treasure each and every "Hello, new day. I'm very happy to see you."

Easter Basket for Daddy

Scott and Monica Heather

Scott and Monica have four children (Kyrston, Michael, Avrial, and Everett) and live in Lake Mills, Wisconsin.

It is two o'clock in the morning on Easter 2013, and an all-too-familiar sound wakes me up. It is Everett, our two-year-old son, who is crying in standard fashion. As I mosey over to the crib, I take notice of the time and think, *Well, at least he made it to two o'clock.* I reach into the crib and begin to rummage around, trying to find my son. Everett is still crying, somewhat less now that he knows I am near, but I cannot find him. I wipe my eyes, put a little more effort into the task of focusing, and search again—still no Everett to be found. My heart begins to thump wildly, but then I feel a huge two-armed hug squeeze my lower leg. I look down, and Everett is snuggling his gorgeous cheeks into the back of my knee.

Everett has three older siblings, so we are very familiar with this exact moment in a child's development—when he figures out mechanically how to maneuver an escape from the crib. This changes everything from the bedtime routine to the implementation of a higher level of baby proofing in the room. With every other kid in the Heather clan,

my wife and I have feared and completely dreaded this day.

Not so with Everett.

Everett has Williams syndrome, and that carries with it a bunch of setbacks, which my wife and I call our "new normal." God works in mysterious ways because this new paradigm has an off-label effect of forcing you to appreciate the little things in a whole new, awe-inspiring light. *Everett got out of his crib!* I screamed in my head. *That's amazing! I need to tell someone!*

I picked him up and started to laugh, and we waltzed around the room. I then quickly woke up my wife and screamed the good news. Jesus rose on the third day and apparently woke Everett up in the process, showing him how to escape life's little cages. It's the only Easter basket that has ever brought me to tears.

My Inspiration
Michele Carlton

Michele lives in upstate New York on the Canadian border with her husband and two children. Michele and her son, Nathan, sing in their church and community and love camping, swimming, biking, and being outdoors.

Nathan was born ten days late, and he looked like a wrinkly old man. By the time he was three months old, he had been rushed to the hospital a half dozen times to reduce a hernia and ended up having surgery and two hernia repairs. He did not sit up or crawl when he should have, and when Nathan was eleven months old, a child developmental specialist told our family that he was mentally challenged (but used a more derogatory term). At the time, we were given no explanations as to his diagnosis and were told that many parents of children with disabilities never receive a diagnosis because the cause is never found.

Nathan had three more surgeries before his second birthday, all for ear tubes. He would have such severe ear infections. His tolerance for pain is extremely high. We made several trips back and forth to the child development specialist for a battery of tests. After several months of poking and prodding, I decided that I didn't need to know what caused his delays. I was done watching him go through these ordeals. So, we gave up trying to find out.

When Nathan turned seven, his pediatrician asked if I had ever found out what caused his delays, and I told him I had not. He convinced me to visit a geneticist, and that is when we finally found out it was Williams syndrome. I was so happy. I finally had a world opened to me that was more defined. I found support that was research-based and also made connections with others who shared our experiences. It  was a relief. Early intervention has made such a difference in Nathan's life.

Nathan is famous. No, not the Nathan's (hotdog) Famous, but Nathan Carlton famous. He is a celebrity wherever we go. We have been to Canada, Virginia Beach, Florida, and other faraway places, and everywhere we go, I can always expect to hear someone holler, "Nathan, how are you?" Like others with Williams syndrome, Nathan has his passions. He loves trains, planes, battleships, fair rides, roller coasters, and television preachers. He has many coffee table books on these subjects, and they are well worn. Nathan reads at about a first-grade level, but he is so resourceful. I kept seeing his books by the computer and couldn't figure out why they were there until I saw him read the letters from his book to type the words into Google. He has learned his way around a computer.

Nathan and I go camping at a local campground every summer. He rides an adult tricycle because of his balance issues. He is a fantastic swimmer, and by the end of the week, everyone there says good-bye to Nathan. He is also a singer. He sings in our church choir. Recently, he was selected to sing the national anthem at Special Olympics Day at our local army post. He sings solos in church and in our community as well.

Nathan is the one person whom you want to meet if you are feeling down. He will put a smile on anyone's face. People ask me, "Does he ever get mad?" The answer is no, Nathan never gets mad. Nathan tells me I am beautiful every day. He even says I look nice when I am wearing my bathrobe. He is the best thing that ever happened to me. I feel so blessed to have been chosen to be his mother. He has taught me patience, love, kindness, forgiveness, and plenty of valuable life lessons.

For me, coming to terms with not having a "normal" child was like going through the stages of grief. I lost the child I had dreamt about. My son would never play team sports, drive a car, live on his own, or do many other things all parents dream for their children. However, once I moved beyond those stages, life became a blessing. I see things now that I would never see if Nathan wasn't with me. I know more about tornadoes and battleships than I ever thought I would. He is truly a gift—a gift that I look forward to sharing with others. I aspire to be like Nathan, who, to me, is the closest thing to perfect in this world of impurities.

The Spice of Life
Mary and Dave Worden

Mary and Dave Worden are from Pewaukee, Wisconsin. They are proud parents of Marcelina and Annelise, who has Williams syndrome.

My wife, Mary, and I have been greatly blessed with two amazing daughters. They have brought, and continue to bring, joy into our lives every day. Our oldest is Marcelina, who is now fifteen and in high school, as hard as it is for us to believe. Our youngest is Annelise, who will be turning thirteen soon. Annelise was diagnosed with Williams syndrome when she was six months old.

Both of our girls certainly have added a tremendous amount of flavor and excitement to our lives, without a doubt. As anyone with a child with Williams syndrome knows, the unique spice that is added to your life is truly amazing, and it is something that we could never have imagined when first finding out so many years ago. Being witness to "Annelise's take" on daily life is a gift that we truly love and appreciate. At this point, we cannot imagine how boring life would be without having the benefit of being able to see it through her unique eyes every single day. Some examples of her view follow:

- Once when listening to music in the car, she proceeded to tell us, "My toes really liked that song."
- During all of the political campaigns one fall, we were getting daily calls like everyone else, and one night Annelise was playing the messages back on the machine. When she cheered across the house like she often does, I asked her what the great news was and she said that someone was calling from a "pumpkin party" and wanted us to call them right back.
- Once when reading a Christmas story that spoke of Jesus as the King of the Jews, Annelise got very excited and said, "That is awesome! I love juice too!"

Like other children with WS, one of the biggest characteristics of Annelise's personality is the constant anticipation of what is coming next. Life, in her eyes, is one big party. She is always looking forward to the next happy event. This ranges from what is for dinner tonight, to her swim lesson tomorrow, to what we are doing this weekend, and everything in between. One time after asking Mom one of these daily one hundred questions, she asked "Mom, is today tomorrow?"

Annelise knows what she likes and what she does not like, and there is no gray whatsoever. She loves many things, including listening to the singer Adele; her dog, Gigi; going fishing; going to parties; reading *Nancy Drew* mysteries; making cookies with Mom; doing anything on the computer; going on vacation; visiting with grandparents and family; getting mail from anyone; getting an email from anyone; going out to dinner; and especially eating pizza or cheeseburgers.

Annelise has taught us much during the last thirteen years. Sometimes these lessons were learned indirectly and sometimes directly.

The very best indirect lesson we have learned was while attending a Williams Syndrome Association conference where one of the speakers provided us with a nugget of knowledge that we have used many times since then: "Every child is on his or her own program." Just this simple statement has brought much comfort, peace, and understanding to us. It has been tremendously helpful to remember this phrase when dealing with educational, behavioral, medical, and even familial issues that have come along during our journey. After all, aren't we all on our own program?

The second lesson is a lesson learned directly from Annelise. Not unlike other children with Williams syndrome, she is challenged daily with things that we take for granted, but yet she has more passion for life and is happier than anyone I know. She reminds us every single day that life does not really have to be as complex as we make it out to be and that it's like the song says: "Don't worry; be happy."

Along with that lesson, we have also learned to live with beautiful simplicity. Life needs to be kept simple. She requires it; our own sanity requires it. We all benefit from breaking down challenges into simpler ones, and the successes come one little step at a time.

This thought brings me to my last lesson. Annelise's first-grade teacher, Mrs. P, constantly told her to slow down and that it was okay to take her time. So for a long time, whenever we tried to move at a pace faster than Annelise could handle, she would remind us, "Mrs. P. says to take my time!" This is where the patience, love, and simplicity needed to kick in—especially when trying to get outside on time for the school bus!

A Whole Lot of Sunshine

Julie Oglesbee

I have spent a few weeks thinking back to what part of my amazing grandson's life I wanted to write about, so here goes. Grayson Jon Oglesbee was born on June 8, 2011. He was a week past his due date and weighed in at five pounds, three ounces. We had no idea at all that he had Williams syndrome until he was about eight weeks old. He had gone for his two-month check-up, and the doctor decided that he had a heart murmur and that it needed to be further checked out. As it is for many families with children with Williams syndrome, this was just the first of many doctors' appointments and one of the first signs that a child may have Williams syndrome. We went to the cardiologist for the usual battery of EKGs and echocardiograms and found out that Grayson had all the signs of Williams syndrome. They said a FISH test needed to be done. We waited for the test results just like everyone does—impatiently, while researching this newfound thing in our lives that was about to impact our hearts and our minds. We went to get the test results and, lo and behold, we were told that Grayson has Williams syndrome.

We went home dumbfounded and started on the journey. We made contacts and connections with *everyone* we could. A friend of ours

happened to know another mom, Michelle, who lives about an hour from us, so we sent her a message asking if we could get in contact with her. We also were put in touch with the Williams Syndrome Association, which has been an amazing help to us. Michelle and the WSA helped guide us in the direction we needed to go.

Now, about this beautiful little boy in our lives—I tried to select one outstanding, amazing story about him that stood out over any other. Wow! That was a difficult task. As he grew and developed and changed and became the little person he is, we realized what a gift we had been given and how our lives would never be the same again. We have been blessed beyond words and, luckily, his health issues have been mere challenges.

He has the "Williams syndrome personality." Grayson is outgoing, spunky, and happy beyond words, and he smiles from ear to ear. He has this little thing that he does that just goes to show how kids with Williams syndrome do have that special, loving, "happy" gene that they talk about. I wish I could include a video instead of a picture so you could see what I mean. But since he was about a year old, he has used his words in one special way. He says, "Hi!" But I don't mean that he just says "hi." He says "hi" to everyone he sees with the biggest smile and a look on his face that you could never imagine. It is the most amazing thing. At almost twenty months now, he still does it. We can be walking through Walmart with Grayson in the cart, and he will wave to every single person who walks by and say, "HI!" If they dare not answer him, he will say it again with an even bigger smile. It's the cutest thing I have ever seen. It's kind of his trademark now. The funny thing is that he is so small—seventeen pounds—that people are mostly shocked, thinking he is too young to be talking, let alone greeting them. In the mall one day recently, Grayson seemed like a beauty pageant winner in a parade, waving to all the onlookers. He warms my heart to no end. I thank God every day that we were given Grayson in our lives.

We are at a point where there are going to be some changes in the dynamic of the family we know. Grayson and his mommy, Elisa, are moving out. This is going to be a huge change for all of us, but I am thinking that it's probably going to affect me the most. I am Grammy JuJu! Now, don't get me wrong—they are only moving about three miles down the road and into a small town that really isn't that far. However, Grayson has become the center of our family's lives for the past two years. There is *nothing* more rewarding to any of us than waking up in the morning and getting that great big smile and "hi," or enjoying that big squeeze when he sees one of us after waking up, or coming home from work and having him there. I love to watch him crawling as fast as he can away from Grandpa, who is on his hands and knees crawling after him and making him laugh. I love having Grayson there every single night, making his rounds to all of us, saying "good night" and "I wuv you!" as he points to his eyes, heart, and then the person he's talking to. I know they need to move to a place of their own and have their own little family, and I know we will still be the center of his life, even in a different home. But, gosh—I will miss that little guy 24-7. He is a loving and caring person who has been created with an exceptional personality and who will always have that special place in my heart. He will always be my little boy with the biggest smile in the whole world.

I trust my daughter's decisions, and she couldn't be a better mom. She always tries to be ahead of the game when it comes to Grayson's care and his future. She has always been the one to research, seek out, and determine what is best for her son. I totally trust that she will always do what is best for Grayson. As a single mom, she has been on this road without a partner to help her, and I give her all the credit in the world. Grayson will always come first in her life. That's why I am so honored that we got to have them under our roof for two whole years and to share in this experience with her. I will always be there for them!

We feel fortunate to have become part of the Williams syndrome community and to have met so many special people with Williams syndrome and their families. We have made special friendships and heard many inspiring stories. We know Grayson will show us the way to go and the way to grow, and we will be learning from him and his friends for the rest of our lives. Thank you, Grayson and Elisa, for this gift. There will be a lifetime of stories for us to tell and share with our Williams syndrome family, and they will be cherished forever.

I Love Bryson City, NC
Debby Shorr Johnson

Debby Shorr Johnson lives in Florida. She enjoys the beach and Florida Springs, walking, natural Florida, and animals. Debby resides with her husband, Bernie, and their children, Mikey and Lily.

When Mikey was about two years old, I decided to volunteer for the Williams Syndrome Association. Through the years, one of the many benefits of doing so has been the wonderful people I have worked with and met along the way.

When chairing a regional conference, there isn't always a lot of time for schmoozing. We have had several conferences down here, thanks to the WSA and other generous donors. But first, let's rewind.

In July 2011, we were on a family vacation, visiting the small town of Bryson City, North Carolina. Our family—Bernie, Mikey, Lily, and me—as well as Lily's two best friends, Sarah and Makenna, were in a little general store on Main Street. It was Camp Johnson that summer, and boy, did we have a blast. A beautiful young woman walked up to Mikey, looked into his eyes, and said, "Hi." He replied, "Hi," and they even maintained eye contact! "I have Williams syndrome," said the young lady. "Wow!" said Mikey. "So do I!" They smiled at each other.

After a brief conversation with the women who accompanied this beautiful young lady (who we learned were her grandmothers and aunt), we discovered that not only did we live only ninety minutes apart in Florida, we had even met before! However, we had to get going. My girls were on the way to tube in the river while Mikey, Bernie, and I planned to play. We said so long, promising to stay in touch.

About a month or so later, we had a WSA regional pool party, and we now had a name—Katelyn and her mom, Katie, joined us for the fun party. We had a pretty big group, and everyone was having a blast when our fun was cut short by a severe thunderstorm that forced us to quickly evacuate. Katie and I did manage to stay in touch via e-mail and decided to meet up again to get everyone together. A short time later, we met at the mall, where Katelyn and Mikey got along amazingly well. We were invited to their home to celebrate a birthday in the family. Katelyn has a sister, Sarah, and a brother named James. We were happy to be a part of the day to celebrate James's birthday.

We were sitting around the table when Katelyn skipped in with a picture or two—you will never believe what we saw. One picture was from a past WSA Regional Conference, and it showed Mikey and Katelyn sitting on a bench with some other friends! Mikey was eight, and Katelyn was nine. A little while later, with her eyes and beautiful smile sparkling, Katelyn invited Mikey to accompany her to her prom in March. Without hesitating and with a huge grin, he replied, "Yes!"

Well, the prom was a whole story in itself, a magical day and night. They like to reminisce and talk about the limo ride, dancing the night away, and how it was one of the most amazing days ever.

This friendship has blossomed, and these two beautiful young adults are there for each other all the time. They laugh together, sing together, talk about their days, and share their hopes and dreams. Katelyn and Mikey are best friends and support each other through good times and bad.

I do think our kids have a special bond. That is why, to this day, I try to plan and support as many WSA regional events as possible. With social networking, they are so easy to plan!

So I give a special thanks to the WSA for supporting regional get-togethers and events. These events help to create lasting friendships, not only between individuals with WS but also between their families.

And that is why you will often hear me say, "I love Bryson City." Lots of people know why—Katie, Terry, Katelyn, James, Sarah, Randi-Anne, GrandMoms, and everyone else in that wonderful family. We love you!

My Daughter

Laura Chesser

Laura Chesser has two daughters, Katelyn and Karalyne. She lives in Michigan and loves to cook, bake, and volunteer.

Katelyn is thirteen years old, soon to be fourteen! Time certainly flies, and I definitely have a teenager on my hands—one who loves activity … away from me (sigh). Katelyn's teenage life includes her Wyldlife group, makeup, horseback riding, TV, makeup, movies, playing board games, cooking and baking in the kitchen, and did I mention makeup? She does *not* love homework but loves school. And she will grab my hand as we walk. Young teenagers … they are quirky creatures.

I am proud of Katelyn and where she is as a young lady. After attending my first Williams Syndrome Association Convention in 2002 in Long Beach, California, I felt I had a well-paved road to travel, a list of specific questions to address with specialists, and a way to set up a meaningful education. I believe with all of my heart that every child learns best while with typical peers in a learning environment (in receiving education, building meaningful relationships, learning adaptable and appropriate behavior skills from each other, transitioning, setting expectations, taking on student responsibility, developing natural supports, etc.). With that mind-set, I work hard to keep an open path so Katelyn can shape her own life.

Katelyn knows herself well, what she likes and dislikes. She is working on figuring out what she expects from others and what others expect from her. We have support from family and friends, which is instrumental in doing what is best for Katelyn. I stand beside her as she is making more decisions for herself, and that is exciting and rewarding. She is shaping her stance in life and school while her awesome personality shines.

Katelyn has been in the general education classroom at school since the beginning. It has been constant work—setting up meaningful education, moving along each year, seeing new faces, and sometimes feeling that we start from square one, especially at big transitional times. She is accommodated mostly very well, sometimes with a lot of conversation. We have had *great* years where the paraprofessional and team had the desire, took guidance, gained an understanding of what types of accommodations were needed, and flew with it. We find it especially true that the "right" accommodations need to wrap a general education curriculum. This is key for Katelyn to gain a meaningful and challenging education. She is in eighth grade and learning eighth-grade curriculum among her friends and classmates.

Middle school is a roller-coaster ride. It is crazy hard to watch Katelyn find her place and maintain her confidence, with lots of hard tears and breaks of good laughter. Seeing her become a more independent young lady *is* wonderful. Knowing I am not the only parent watching this difficult rite of passage is helpful. Friends and family share the same types of stories, so I know Katelyn is not alone. And for the families coming around this middle school corner of life, know that the hard stuff is *normal*. She is continuing to find herself by trying sports and activities, exploring learning opportunities in and out of school, and enjoying her "crew," the Wyldlife group.

So with all of that said, here are a few of my favorite clips of Katelyn's personality and abilities.

Animal Stories (Her Younger Years)

Katelyn loves the nature channels and anything to do with watching animals interact. One of the things we have enjoyed since she was very young is watching a quiet animal movie and giving words to their interactions. We simply make a story out of animals' interacting with one another. We began this game when Katelyn followed my lead one day when she was maybe two years old. She began adding funny animal noises, and gradually we created a plot. Still to this day, we do this whenever we have the opportunity. It's fun. Sometimes, we turn competitive and rewind over and over, trying for more dramatic and silly narration. The winner is the one who gets the most giggles. (Caution: we have found that doing this activity in a movie theater annoys people.)

To Guard or Not to Guard: That Is the Question

Katelyn decided to play basketball during her seventh-grade year. As she progressed in getting more comfortable with actually playing, she started scrimmaging at practice. The coach approached me after one practice, laughing. I knew this was going to be good. The coach said that Katelyn "was in rare form today and hilarious, as always."

The coach put Katelyn into scrimmage against a teammate, one who wouldn't take her down on the court. (FYI, seventh-grade basketball is a full-contact sport—seriously! This made Katelyn a bit leery.) The coach told Katelyn to make sure this teammate did not get the ball. *Okay*, I thought. *Easy enough.* Katelyn had a job to do.

My daughter respectfully said, "Okay, Coach!" with absolute determined gusto. She then called the assigned teammate to come over (enthusiastically) and proceeded to walk the teammate across the gymnasium to a faraway corner of the court. Katelyn told the teammate to stay right there and don't move. She emphasized the "don't move" part with her hands to give it dramatic meaning. The teammate said "okay" and stayed put. (I am sure she was a bit confused.) My daughter walked away, ready to "play" ball.

The coach saw what happened and, while keeping her laughter under control, told Katelyn she was to keep the ball away from her teammate while actually *playing* the game. Katelyn walked away saying, "Okay, Coach," shaking her head and laughing. The coach released the teammate from the designated corner, once the coach was able to pull herself together.

The best part about being included on the school basketball team? Her coach and teammates saw Katelyn's personality, humor, and willingness to try. She absolutely shined.

I find it amazing that education staff sometimes discredits Katelyn's ability to present. She loves to make people laugh and inform them of important things, and she takes presenting very seriously. The best part is that presenting combines speech, language, reading, writing, organizing, preparing, and practicing—what wonderful skills and abilities to bring together. She loves to speak about topics of interest, such as animals, friends, experiences, and people who make a difference. A few of her most memorable are the human heart, Dr. Seuss, and gibbon monkeys. When Katelyn presented on Dr. Seuss, she had to dress up. She picked the costume, I painted her face, and she walked into school as the Cat in the Hat. The younger kids saw her and were all excited, pointing and giggling. Katelyn grew two inches that day.

Katelyn utilizes her computer for larger presentations. When she is involved in a group presentation, it is a full collaborative effort. Each classmate will insert his or her portion, often putting personal pictures and cool animations onto Katelyn's computer. They enjoy presenting together with the added bonus of her computer, which was a very big deal in school. One thing you can count on—Katelyn loves to put emotion into things she speaks about, especially in front of an audience. And, watch out, because she has no problem adding surprises.

The speech and language therapist played a big role in her presentation, helping Katelyn with vocabulary and language skills (and not just focusing on articulation). Katelyn started presenting in third grade for current events, as did all the other classmates. Teachers were pleasantly surprised, at first. I just smiled and said, "Of course, she's good at it."

Chapter 5

Gifts

Everyone is special in his or her own way, and it seems that people with Williams syndrome are special in many ways that are increasingly lacking from society at large. Perhaps this is why, given the chance, their impact is so profound. One wide smile for a stranger can change his whole day; one unsolicited hug for a struggling teacher can give her the comfort she needs to keep going. But these simple acts, while valuable, are not the whole picture. What is remarkable about those with Williams syndrome is their apparent ability to tune into people's needs for those smiles and hugs—and deliver them right on time.

A Social Butterfly

Karen L. Young

Karen Young has two sons and lives in Michigan. She loves writing, reading, and spending time with her four grandsons.

An adorable little girl named Bailey Stack came into my life about ten years ago. She was about five at the time and helped create one of those "aha" moments in my life. Since I am going on Medicare in two months, I have lived long enough to have a lot of "aha" moments. But this one really sticks in my mind, all because of Bailey.

My son, Rob Young, had fallen in love with Bailey's aunt, Tammy Wilhite. I went to a celebratory event at the Wilhite family home to honor Tammy for graduating from college. When I arrived at the Wilhite house, Rob and Tammy were not there yet. They were the only two people I knew. Tammy's parents, Bob and Kathy, were busy putting last-minute touches on the dinner, so  I was greeted at the door by Bailey. She was so happy to see me and to meet "Rob's mom." Remember, she was just five years old, but she took over the situation like a social butterfly. She made me feel so welcome and at ease. I was really happy to be there. I didn't feel "alone" anymore. In fact, Bailey saw to it that everyone who came in the door knew that "Rob's mom" was there and they needed to come into the living room and meet me.

It was several days later that I was told about Williams syndrome and the fact that Bailey was born with it. I had never heard of it, and—I will be honest—I still don't know a lot about it. I have just felt it necessary to support the Association in any way I can, for Bailey's sake. I want to take her at face value and not fit her into categories.

She was there for me at a moment in time when I really needed her, and I know she didn't even realize it.

Throughout these ten years, I have witnessed the trials that Bailey has gone through because of her health. Yet, every time I see her, she is the one trying to make me feel at home and comfortable. She has excitedly greeted me with, "Hi, Rob's mom. I'm so glad you're here," as though she were waiting solely for my appearance. Across a crowded room or crowded backyard, wherever it may be, I will hear Bailey calling to me. Of course, after Rob and Tammy had Noah, "Rob's mom" became "Grandma Karen." And, honestly, I don't feel I have arrived until I hear that "Hi, Grandma Karen" and get that special hug from Bailey.

Bailey handles this syndrome with the utmost grace and charm and works very hard at everything she does. I will *never* forget that first encounter with her and how at ease she made me feel at an uncomfortable moment in time.

Williams Syndrome: Insight and Gratitude
Mary Fallon

Mary Fallon has just retired after a long and highly rewarding career as a teacher on both the university and secondary school levels. She has taught Spanish, English literature, and writing, which is her area of special expertise. She has also published many articles and has acted as a ghost writer and editor. Recently, Mary worked in collaboration with a student from Niger to publish a book comparing his experience in the United States with his experience as a nomadic member of the Tuareg people in the Sahara.

"You know, Julianne, as a society, we really put very narrow parameters around what we consider to be the potential of our children. It's actually amazing. Here we are. We're educators, and still we confine ourselves to a very narrow understanding of the gifts and the possible contributions each can make to our society and to our humanity."

I was speaking to my colleague, a fellow teacher in the summer program I was teaching at a private prep school in New Hampshire. As I stood at my desk gazing out the window at the lush lakeshore that bounded this rolling, green campus, my mind was caught up in a quote I had read in a book on Zen the previous evening. The expression "loving kindness" was still echoing in my consciousness. I believed in kindness. In fact, although I often came up short in this area, I did hold it as a goal for living, a goal that could give direction and meaning to my life.

Julianne, who had been working on her laptop, looked up at me ready to listen to my reflections. What a good and accommodating friend!

Caught up in my new awareness, I began to tell her about the deeply instructive experience I had had the previous winter when I attended the funeral of my older sister, JoAnne, who had died unexpectedly from a massive stroke in early February.

I remember the first time I saw Ray, my great-nephew and JoAnne's grandson, on that sad, mournful visit. As he walked with his family behind the casket, I noticed his tousled, light brown hair above the wire-rim spectacles he wore. As the family moved toward the entrance of the funeral home, I focused on Ray. He wore a satiny light blue tie, which he lifted to his face to daub his eyes. Ray embraced his sorrow. He accepted the enormity of what was happening around us so openly. I was so drawn to his open expression of the grief that I felt a release, and my eyes began to tear.

As we entered the building and hung our coats on a rack just outside the parlor, there were whispered "hellos" and brief hugs shared among family and friends. But overall the sense of strangeness and disbelief was almost palpable. Why were we here? Could this be so? We streamed into the main room, and I saw it there before us across a wide expanse of chairs and open space—a shiny, copper-colored casket draped with an effusion of multicolored flowers and a wide banner that read "Mother." I stood motionless.

And then I felt it—a warm touch. I opened my eyes and looked to my side, and there was Ray. "Are you sad, Great-Aunt Mary?" I looked down into his wide, caring eyes and felt him pat my hand. "Yes, Ray, I am sad." He patted my hand again, and I stooped down to look directly into his face. "I'm sorry you are sad, Great-Aunt Mary." Again he patted my hand, and I took his in both of mine. "Thank you so much for coming over, Ray. It helps me to talk to you. I know you care." I said. "Yes, Great-Aunt Mary. I am sorry you are sad." His brow furrowed with concern, and his eyes focused on mine. I held his hand for a brief moment as he looked at me tenderly, and then I stood up to allow him to return to his family. "I will come back, Great-Aunt Mary," he promised me before he turned away.

The next day, we returned to the chapel for high mass in memory of JoAnne. I had been asked by my niece to read a text from the Old Testament right after the priest was finished. It was a passage on the good wife. I carried it to the front of the chapel with me and slipped into a side pew. *I can't do this!* The thought cut sharply through my chest. *I can't do this! I can't get up there and read. I can't even climb up to the altar. I can't.* I could feel my face draining of color. I could feel the coldness in my hands. I felt woozy.

Luckily someone had noticed my distress. One of the staff hurried over to me and grasped my hand. "Are you all right?" she asked with concern. "I can't do it," I answered, with a gentle sob. "I can't read this." She patted my hand firmly. "Yes, you can," she assured me. "You can do it. Right now you have to breathe." I was able to step out of the pew and circle the chapel twice, inhaling deeply and finally returning to my place to hear the priest's final words.

Then, it was my turn, and I walked into the aisle and climbed the wooden stairs that led to the pulpit. I stepped up to the lectern, but before I could begin, I prefaced the reading with, "I cannot imagine a reading that could be more meaningful, more fitting for my sister than this. If anyone was the good wife and mother, it was my sister, JoAnne." I managed to read the text in a steady, solid tone. I spoke the final words with a sense of completion and gratitude. I had done it. Suddenly, I felt a shattering force of remembrance and loss cut through my body. Could she be gone? Could this be real?

I could feel the weakness in my knees. Fortunately, I caught the gaze of a young man in a dark suit. I mouthed the words, "Help. Please help," as I backed away from the pulpit. Ready and responsive, the young man recognized my need and climbed the steps and clasped my arm. He led me across the polished wood floor and down the steps. When we reached the bottom, he gently turned me toward the pew at the side of the chapel.

However, I was greeted by another presence. I looked down at Ray. With his hand outstretched, he said, "Come with me, Great-Aunt Mary. Come and sit with us."

He led me to his family, who was seated in the second pew from the front. After letting go of my hand, he folded himself at the end of the pew. I rested my hand on the back of the bench in front of us, and Ray raised his hand and gave me a gentle pat. Salvation. I felt the warm glow of belonging to all who surrounded me. And I knew why I felt that glow. I was, after all, sitting next to an angel.

Final Note:

I am so grateful to have the opportunity to write about Ray. He certainly did touch me at the funeral. He was so in tune with what people were feeling, so empathic, and so open to reaching out. After the funeral, I kept telling people how deeply he had inspired me. He actually gave me comfort in my own experience of loss.

Here we are, seeing children with special needs as somehow needing to be "fixed." And there I was telling people that Ray seemed to have a special "genius," a special gift, a profound empathy and ability to reach out in love—to be open to love and connection to others. He was not intimidated by the social self-consciousness that often holds us back but rather demonstrated a deep trust in the connections we share.

The Smartest One-and-a-Half-Year-Old I Know

Dan Coggshall

Dan Coggshall is currently wrapped around the fingers of two little girls, Charlotte and Emmy. He lives with his amazing wife, Vanessa, in New Jersey and loves reading good fiction, bumbling his way through home improvement projects, and watching football and baseball when his girls will let him.

Emmy makes this face when she's really happy. She scrunches up her nose, widens her smile, squints her eyes, and goes, "Ha!" She knows I love it, and she invites me into her joy every time she does it.

When Emmy wants you to hold her, all she does is outstretch her little arms, bounce with her whole body, and flash expecting eyes in your

direction. She'll dive right out of your arms into the arms of another, if you're not careful. She knows there is not a person with an ounce of love in his or her heart who wouldn't grab her right away.

On numerous occasions, in the time that it takes me to swipe my credit card and sign the little keypad thing, Emmy has made a friend for life out of the cashier.

Emmy is the smartest one-and-half-year-old I know. Sure, she's a bit behind on her milestones. She can talk but only has a few words. She can walk but mostly stumbles. But she can work the room like no other.

I come from a family that places a high importance on education, and I've worked for the last fourteen years to help high-achieving kids get into selective colleges by doing better on their SATs. So, you'd think that I would measure someone's intelligence by how high he or she can score on a test or whether or not he or she could get into Harvard.

(Actually, in my family, the ultimate sign of intelligence is getting into Harvard and then turning them down, because why would anyone want to be around a bunch of people who go to Harvard?)

Before Emmy, I have to admit: that was how I looked at it. But Emmy has taught me another, far more important dimension of intelligence. In this life, to get what you want, someone generally has to allow you to have it. Getting someone to like you is often more important than getting the right answer. Winning people over is usually the path to success in this society. Social smarts are often more important than book smarts. I think it took Emmy to teach me this because I have spent most of my life trying to use book smarts to compensate for social smarts.

When she was first diagnosed, it was hard not to start to take a tally of everything we assumed she probably wouldn't do: go to college, drive a car, or live independently. By extension, I couldn't help but take a tally of everything I probably wouldn't be able to do: travel abroad, coach her soccer team, or enjoy my retirement living alone with my wife.

We've learned since then that there are no limits on what Emmy can do. Sure, doctors tried to tell us that. Parents of other children with Williams syndrome tried to tell us that. Individuals with Williams tried to show us that. But it was Emmy who has taught us never to doubt her and to never lower our expectations.

First, Emmy started hitting some of the goals and milestones that we assumed were too lofty for her, based on everything we had read. Sure, she hit them a bit behind her older sister but still well within the typical range. Then, she started surprising us by doing things that we read she wouldn't, like eating anything and everything, as if she were preparing for the Nathan's Famous Hot Dog Eating Contest. Then, we started noticing all the things that Emmy was doing earlier and better than typical children.

At twenty-one months old, Emmy wins people over better than anyone her age (and far better than I do at my age). Every day at school, kids from different classes drag their parents into Emmy's room to say good-bye to Emmy. Complete strangers have purchased toys and given them to her within minutes of meeting her. When Emmy does drive one day, I guarantee she will be able to charm her way out of every ticket.

This is not accidental. Sure, Emmy is cute, but a lot of kids are cute. Sure, caring adults who know she has special needs treat her a little more nicely, but she is winning people over who have absolutely no idea that Emmy is anything but typical. This is Emmy flexing her brain muscles.

She's learned, through keen observation and plenty of trial and error, exactly what gets a smile out of her dad, a hug out of her mom, and more time with her sister's toys. She applies this knowledge like the genius she is with everyone she meets, especially those who have exhibited gift-giving behavior in the past, like Grandma Aggie and Aunt Emily.

And this is not just a proud father thinking his kids are the best, no matter what. Emmy has plenty of weaknesses to offset these strengths, just like any other kid. And this is also not just a proud Williams dad thinking that his kid is the best Williams kid there is, because there are spreadsheets of data in Louisville, Kentucky, to confirm that Emmy's behavior is typical among other kids with Williams.

I have learned from Emmy to never lower my expectations and never assume she can't do something. My goal with both of my children, thanks to Emmy's instruction, is to find their strengths and help them exploit those strengths to find success, however they want to measure it. For Emmy, that path could lead anywhere, including Harvard, but it will probably be the power of her interview, and not her Math SAT scores, that gets her there. The one thing I can tell already is that she'd be smart enough to turn them down.

Walking in Williams Syndrome

Jennifer Peruso

Jennifer Peruso lives in Matamoras, Pennsylvania. She is married and teaches fourth grade. She sits on the board for the Center for Developmental Disabilities in Milford, Pennsylvania, and loves spending her free time with her family. Her greatest joy, however, is being Gabriel's mother.

Being a mother to a child with special needs garners pity from some people. I know there are people who think, *That poor girl.* I have seen it in their eyes. I find people shaking their heads when I tell them that Williams syndrome occurs in 1 in 10,000 births, as if I have been robbed of something, as if my life would have been better off if I had a "normal" baby, as if Gabriel is "broken" in some way. They are happy that they are not the ones in my situation. Usually, after meeting Gabriel, they change their minds because most people see the charming, sweet, and loving boy that I see. They see the boy who is far from broken and is more free than most of us will ever hope to be in our lives. However, I still wonder if there is a part of their minds that still feels pity for what we didn't have—a quiet place in their hearts and minds that questions how we could be truly happy with a child with special needs. That notion is foreign to me, as I could not feel more blessed and honored to be Gabriel's mom on any given day. There is no pity in my mind, just miracles that occur daily.

People mean well—they truly do—but they really just don't understand. They don't understand that my life has been blessed beyond measure by a little boy with Williams syndrome. They don't understand that I would go through all of it again and again to have the privilege of spending my life in the presence of pure joy and overwhelming happiness. They don't understand that to be loved by someone with Williams syndrome is to know the true meaning of pure love for the first time. They don't understand that people with Williams syndrome live in the moments of life, in whatever emotion they are having, in a very *real* way—an experience that few of us have ever felt because we spend so much time worrying about what other people are thinking. They don't understand that I am the one who is blessed, and the blessing of my son will never be lost on me.

The beginnings of Williams syndrome and its impact on our lives were not beautiful, however. It was extremely difficult. There were many times during Gabriel's infancy when I felt sorry for myself and thought I would never survive. I thought I had been given a burden too great, that motherhood would never bring me the joy I had hoped for. He was very sick and colicky and cried all the time. In addition, he never slept. I wasn't sure what the future held, so I lived day by day.

However, at around a year-and-a-half, things shifted a bit, and Gabriel started to emerge. I began to see this sweet and smiley toddler coming to life. In that toddler I saw hope—hope for him, hope for me, for what life could be like for Gabriel. We still did not know at that point that he had Williams syndrome; we just knew there was "something." Once we discovered that Williams syndrome was "it," we were truly able to move forward. Gabriel has done really well. He has received numerous therapies all along. He went to a very specialized preschool program, he has amazing specialists, and we have a terrific family support system, as well as great friends. Gabriel's life is a very full one, with amazing people who support and cheer for him every step of the way.

Gabriel is currently in kindergarten. He spends part of his day in the life skills room, where he receives his reading and math instruction one on one. He spends a good portion of the day with typical peers. He is initiating play and enjoys interacting with his friends. However, he is behind his peers both socially and academically. I have a feeling that will always be the case to some degree. He receives therapies in and out of school and is making progress daily. He has some sensory issues to work on, and his attention span can be a challenge. He loves playing in his sandbox and digging for worms. He loves bulldozers and backhoes. He loves a good party and spending time with his family. He loves any opportunity to meet and chat with new people, despite only starting to talk two years ago. He loves playing outside and watching elk and weed whacker videos online. I look forward to meeting each new challenge and helping Gabriel reach his full potential, whatever that may be.

Being Gabriel's mom has taught me so much. It has taught me patience and persistence. It has taught me the meaning of beauty, true beauty in a moment. It has taught me to stand still and experience that moment, as he does, with all that I am. He has taught me what real joy looks and feels like. He has humbled me and made me feel true gratitude down to the core of who I am. He has inspired me by his strength and will to prevail over small triumphs and large ones. He has shown me what life is all about and brought a light and richness to my life, which I did not know was missing. I have never felt sadness because Gabriel has Williams syndrome; I have always felt like it has blessed us in so many extraordinary ways. To know Gabriel is to love him. My only wish as his mom is for the world to give him a chance to let his light shine, for those people who shake their head in pity to stop and spend some time basking in Gabriel's light and to give him a chance to share his gifts with them. His gifts are plenty, and I can't wait to see how his beautiful life continues to unfold.

Our Favorite Teacher

Lisette Y. Orellana

Lisette Orellana is an advocate for her children and young families with children with special needs in her community. She blogs on a regular basis and enjoys spending time with her family and friends. She lives in Maryland with her two kids, Gina and Jeremy, and their mischievous cat, Luciano.

I worry a lot about my son. Perhaps I worry for selfish reasons. I was a teen mom, who by the age of seventeen was a mother to two babies. A senior in high school, I had yet to find out about Jeremy's diagnosis of Williams syndrome. When he was diagnosed at age two, life changed for my daughter and me. We embarked on a journey in which both of us would learn a great deal about acceptance, patience, and, most importantly, unconditional love.

Through the years, Gina and I have enjoyed having Jeremy in our lives. Gina is a great sister to him, and Jeremy brings much joy to our family. He's an amazing child with an abundance of kindness and respect and a hunger for life and learning. One thing that Jeremy does well is teach each and every one he meets that he doesn't have any limits and that it is us (the "mainstreamers") who set limitations on what we do. This lesson came to us just last year.

Jeremy, who is nine years old, attends a special education program at a different school. Gina, at ten years old, has seen how independent he is and how well he does on his own. After all, there is no bigger social butterfly than Mr. Jeremy himself. We had been having various meetings and conversations about inclusion to mainstream classes because he seems to get along so well with other children. It was time to see if he was socially mature enough to be around the mainstream students. It was decided at one of his IEP meetings that he would be going to physical education with the typical second-grade class. I had completely forgotten to tell Jeremy that morning that he would be going to PE with another class. I'm glad I didn't because, that night, he came home with the biggest smile on his face.

"Mom, thank you so much for signing me up for that special PE class! I had the best time! I know I'm in special ed, but that's okay. I can do a lot." He did so well for the remainder of the year that, as we planned the next year, the teacher suggested that he could take part in their "Buddy Program." Being part of this program meant that Jeremy would be allowed to go into a mainstream classroom in  the mornings and during lunch and recess, and he could also go to any specials with that mainstream classroom. Needless to say, he is doing wonderfully and has shown his teachers and myself how capable he is at adapting and defying adversity. During this transition, he is showing us that no one wants to be successful more than him. He's become a role model in class and has really been a role model for Gina and me.

Jeremy is a true example of "Ask and you shall receive." I know you can relate when I say that plenty of times we want to do something or know something, but we are too afraid to ask. Not Jeremy. Perhaps it is in part due to Williams that he has no fear of strangers, but then again his personal charm cannot be overlooked. He proved this summer that all you have to do is ask. We went on a trip to Portland. For our first layover, I was busy carrying our bags, and once I stepped off the plane to go into the walkway, I realized that neither he nor Gina were behind me! My heart skipped a beat, and I quickly began calling them. I heard a tiny voice coming from the cockpit … and they were there, with the captain. Jeremy had asked the pilot of the plane if he could see where they "drive" the plane, and the captain and crew gladly allowed them to go in and take a seat. The captain kindly explained what the buttons did and allowed us to take pictures! Gina and I would have never had the courage to go back there and ask, but Jeremy showed us that the worst that can happen is someone simply saying no. Lucky for us, in this case, we walked out with a memory of a lifetime.

This trip was also important to me. I worried a lot about Jeremy because I thought about how the plane might hurt his ears, how he might not tolerate the long flight—the list goes on. I truly feared for how he would do. It was the complete opposite. He was a great brother and a great companion to me, making the trip and flight easier. Gina has really bad anxiety, and he was such a good support to her in keeping her distracted. It made me realize there are no limitations to him, and he is quite exceptional.

Gina and I have quickly learned that *we* live in Jeremy's world. Thanks to him, I have learned that it doesn't matter that I was a young single mom; it matters that I have been successful at being the mother he and his sister deserve. It was most definitely an eye opener, and we are so thankful to continue to receive life lessons from our own ray of sunshine—Jeremy.

Just a Couple Cupcakes

Renee Rodriguez

Renee Rodriguez has one son, Eddie. She lives in Sugar Grove, Illinois, and loves running, baking cupcakes, and spending time with her husband, son, and dogs.

It has been said that you get more out of life by giving than receiving. I am a true believer in that! I do not have a child with Williams syndrome or a family member who is affected by it. But I do have a few new friends whom Williams syndrome has touched in one way or another.

In 2011, I had a side business making cupcakes for friends and family, and it was something I truly enjoyed. As time passed, it became more difficult to keep up with the demand for my cupcakes, especially while

 also working full-time. Then I had a revelation. I needed to donate my sweet creations instead of selling them. This was the perfect opportunity to give to others. And while I wasn't quite sure how I would start this donation strategy, I knew I would know when the time was right.

On a Friday night in June of the same year, my husband and I were watching TV and tuned in to a *20/20* special on ABC. The show featured children with Williams syndrome. As we watched, I shed a few tears and kept telling my husband, Tony, that I had found the perfect place to share my cupcakes.

I had not heard of Williams syndrome before, even though I had worked with children with learning disabilities while I attended community college many years before. After the show ended, it was all I could think about that weekend. When Monday morning arrived, I turned to the Internet to find out how I could volunteer.

After a few months of researching the Williams Syndrome Association website, I came across an event that was coming up in my area. It was the Midwest summer picnic. I immediately reached out to Ashley, and she was very receptive to my request. While she was not able to attend the picnic that year, she told me about the Williams Syndrome Holiday Bowling Party that takes place each December in my community. She said I could assist at the party and assured me that it would be a memorable experience. She expressed that I would surely be moved, and the children would touch my life. She shared how the children's excitement would warm the room, especially when greeted with the special visit from Santa Claus.

So, on December 13, 2011, armed with twenty-two six packs of cupcakes, Tony and I headed to the bowling party. From the moment Tony and I entered the bowling alley, we were welcomed by families. The children were amazing—so beautiful, loving, and very inquisitive. While they did not know us, it did not stop them from offering the grand reception we received. We were approached by a few of the parents, who would ask, "Which child is yours?" and we would respond, "We don't have a child with Williams. We just want to help out." I am sure to a few parents this sounded odd, but they were gracious and receptive. Our day was perfect. At the end of the party, Tony and I handed out my cupcakes to each family. The gratitude was heartwarming. It was a perfect day!

We knew that this was where we needed to donate time and cupcakes whenever possible. In May of 2012, we put on our walking shoes for the three-mile walk in Morris, Illinois, to benefit Williams syndrome. In August, we participated in the picnic. These experiences have changed our lives, and the memories will be with us forever.

On December 15, 2012, we participated in our second annual Williams Syndrome Bowling Party. We were so excited since, this time, our son, Eddie, was able to attend. Again, we packed twenty-two six packs of cupcakes and a few for dessert. The children gravitated toward Eddie as soon as we arrived. They happily questioned him about his favorite color, band, and hobbies. The kids welcomed him as if he were an old friend. And it wasn't just the children who were amazing; it was their families too. As people arrived, a woman approached me and said, "Hello Renee! How are you?" I was so surprised because I had not seen her in a year, and she remembered me. When I shared how impressed I was that she remembered me, she said, "How could I forget you? You gave us those delicious cupcakes!"

My husband, son, and I are so blessed to be part of these events and programs for Williams syndrome. These children radiate beauty, love, and caring to everyone they meet. When I think back to the *20/20* special (as I often do), I think of a comment Chris Cuomo made: "If we all just had a little Williams syndrome in us, the world would be a better place."

I strive to be a better person because of what I have learned from those who have been touched by Williams syndrome. This is how Williams syndrome has affected my life. I have a reason to make cupcakes and donate them at every chance I can. My goal is to donate each and every year. I am looking forward to helping out at the Midwest walk this May and also hope to head games at the picnic in the summer.

Thank you, Williams syndrome, for touching my life in the most beautiful way possible!

"Angels Among Us"
Melissa J. Baer

Melissa Baer lives in Missouri. She and her husband, Jeff, have been blessed with three lovely daughters—Emelia, Ashlyn, and Elise—two frisky cats, and one adorable puppy. Melissa enjoys traveling, reading, writing, and spending time with family and friends.

Certain songs just make me cry. It does not matter where I am, what I'm doing, or how many times I have heard the song. One song that has always moved me is entitled "Angels Among Us." The song as a whole has an inspirational message, but it is the chorus that really touches my soul:

> "I believe there are angels among us
> Sent down to us from somewhere up above
> They come to you and me in our darkest hours
> To show us how to live
> To teach us how to give
> To guide us with the light of love"

Being a Christian my entire life, I had read about angels in the Bible, but I hadn't spent much time contemplating them. I believed they existed but had never examined their presence or purpose—that is, until my second daughter, Ashlyn, was born and forever changed my life.

My little angel was born in May 2002. From the first time I held her, I sensed that something was different. With her curly blonde hair and dazzling blue eyes, she did not favor her daddy, older sister, or me. I fell in love with her, even though she cried incessantly and was the cause of extreme sleep deprivation. Her pediatrician suggested that we meet with a pediatric cardiologist to investigate what we thought at the time was a harmless heart murmur. Within two days, Ashlyn had an entire team of doctors at our local children's hospital. At five weeks old, she was diagnosed with Williams syndrome. The cardiologist predicted that open-heart surgery would be imminent. The geneticist assured us that Williams syndrome was not necessarily a life-threatening condition and that, in his experience, children who have it often become complete joys to their families. With that sketchy bit of information and future appointments scheduled, we were sent home to begin our new journey.

Shocked, I returned home in a complete fog and remained in a depressed state for some time. I had to bond with my baby all over again. I felt as if I were being forced into a fraternity to which I had no desire to belong. Friends moved on with their fast-paced lives, while therapists and doctors became my new confidants. My career was placed on the back burner. I was, in truth, overwhelmed and felt completely alone. Questions plagued me: Would Ashlyn need surgery? Would my other children love her unconditionally or grow to resent her? Would my marriage survive? Would Ashlyn form friendships and be accepted by others? Would she be successful in school and have the opportunity to participate in extracurricular activities?

Thankfully, faith and time have a way of healing the spirit. As Ashlyn's health and development progressed, my attitude also improved. My anxieties and fears subsided, and my questions were eventually answered. Much to her cardiologist's surprise, Ashlyn's heart issues miraculously improved to the point of avoiding surgery. I fell crazy in love with my angel. The blessings she has brought into my life are countless.

I have learned to cherish the new friends I have made along this journey—beautiful people I never would have met without Ashlyn. I recognize the incredible blessing the WSA family has been. I have also found contentment in a new career path. My marriage has been enriched, as my husband and I have learned to lean on each other for patience and strength. My other two daughters absolutely adore Ashlyn and are growing into wonderful young ladies full of compassion, kindness, and acceptance of others. Ashlyn has not only been accepted but is also loved and adored by her family and friends. She has many friends of all ages who appreciate her kindness, charm, wit, and quirky humor. Her smile and happiness are contagious and bring joy to others. She enjoys school and is a wonderful student who brings a splash of fun and cheer to her classroom. She has an active life and participates in Special Olympics track and field events, an after-school running club, and a cheerleading team. Ashlyn is a unique person with a true gift for making others happy. We are blessed to have this incredible little girl in our family!

Why do I call Ashlyn "my little angel"? She is quite honestly angelic. I do not mean she is perfect. Rather, she has her struggles and challenges in life and always will. Her anxieties often get the better of her. She sometimes struggles to respond appropriately in specific situations, thereby leading to confusion and embarrassment. Even when she does understand the rules and knows exactly what she should do or say, she often lacks the self-control to deliver the desired results. She gets frustrated and then becomes upset with herself for disappointing others. Ashlyn requires more patience and energy than I sometimes have to give. However, I have learned to accept her issues, along with the many blessings she has to offer.

When I describe Ashlyn as angelic, I mean that she perfectly fits the description of angels as portrayed in the lyrics of "Angels Among Us." I truly believe that Ashlyn and others with Williams syndrome are sent down from God as gifts to all of us. They are angelic in their relationships and are examples of how to treat others. Their inherent kindness and purity of spirit are things I continue to strive for but of which I always fall short. Their positive outlook and overall happiness with life are contagious.

Ashlyn's kindness at school is obvious based on the number of friends she has. I find notes in her backpack from classmates telling her how pretty, kind, and funny she is. She has numerous BFWOPs (Best Friends With Older Persons). The principal, staff, school nurse, bus driver, custodians, teachers—she knows them all by name and considers them all her BFWOPs. She enthusiastically skips to the bus every morning with a "Good morning, all!" and I can hear her greet each child as the door closes.

Ashlyn is brought to tears when one of her classmates is being disciplined. She worries terribly when a friend or family member is sick. She speaks to complete strangers in Walmart, introducing herself and commenting on something she likes about them. Ashlyn makes friends while waiting in line for a ride at Disney World, even if the family does not speak English. Her smile and kind tone are sufficient. She sings and prays louder than the rest of the congregation at church as her voice is lifted in praise. She rocks her Elvis and Michael Jackson montage each night in the shower as she entertains her puppy, Toodles.

Ashlyn is her sisters' biggest fan. She screams the loudest when her older sister, Emelia, nails her side leap in a dance routine and when her little sister, Elise, gets a hit and runs to first base. She convincingly tells each relative that he or she is her favorite. How many times a day does Ashlyn hug me and tell me she loves me? She always seems to pick the moments I need it the most, as if she can sense my need for love. She truly makes everyone feel like he or she is the most awesome person she knows.

A wise person once said to me, "If only I could have a pocket-sized Ashlyn to keep in my purse and pull out when I need an infusion of happiness." How truly blessed I am to have the real deal in my life!

Advice, Perspective, and a Teacher's Letter
Tiffany Crabtree

Tiffany and Justin have two incredible boys, Sam and Isaac. They like to call their hometown (Jackson Hole, Wyoming) paradise. In the summer, they enjoy camping, paddle boarding on String Lake, picking huckleberries, hiking, waterskiing, and doing anything else they can do outdoors. In the long winter months, they ski and shovel snow into gigantic piles, to play on and build forts in, while watching out for locals (moose, elk, coyotes, great horned owls, wolves, and buffalo).

Isaac has given us a perspective that we never knew possible. In the beginning, we had no idea of the trials to come and no clue as to the power of a child's spirit. Isaac has brought to us a strength we did not know we had and enriched our lives more than words can describe. Our son got a rough start at life; he was premature and weighed in at a whopping three pounds, fifteen ounces when we took him home. He seemed to be a happy kid at first, and we were truly happy in our ignorance. Isaac was not growing very fast, and we thought it was just the way he was. Our illusion was shattered when, at thirty days old, Isaac suffered from double incarcerated hernias and endured what turned out to be the first of three Life Flights he would ultimately take.

From that point on, we realized that Isaac would not be like his older, "typical" brother in many respects. He was physically behind at a young age. Now he loves to play and smile and run all over the neighborhood, but it took tremendous effort on the part of many caring and outstanding supporters to make that happen. Our family has realized several times the importance of taking a break from doctors and therapies in order to maintain a "normal" life; however, I do believe that without early intervention and occupational therapy, Isaac would not have made the great strides that he did early on. Although we still have a long road ahead, we are proud of the progress that we, as a family, have made.

Now that Isaac is eight, we realize how important it is for him to be part of his community. We are currently working with his IEP team so he can have a recreational therapist outside of school. Once Isaac learns appropriate behavior in a specific setting, it sticks with him. A few summers ago, the therapist took him to the post office every day and practiced how to behave in that setting. Then she made him a book about how the post office looks and wrote a social story to go along with it. This was a very simple task but has made a world of difference; Isaac can now walk into the post office without experiencing a breakdown.

Airports and grocery stores are our biggest challenges. We have learned that if Isaac can have a gadget to play with while grocery shopping, we can make it through the store. We will eventually work on getting through the store with no electronics. We have to prep Isaac for days beforehand about taking a flight (what it will sound like and what it will look like) because air travel causes anxiety for typical people, and Isaac is no different. We often find ourselves in uncomfortable conversations explaining why Isaac talks throughout the flight—it is his only way to cope. Having a dog has also helped with some of Isaac's anxiety.

Isaac is thriving at school because of the structured environment. He meets with his favorite teacher every morning to set his personal goals for the day and determine what rewards (shredding paper, sharpening pencils, lunch with his friends in the classroom, or extra computer time) he will be able to earn if he achieves those goals. This motivates him and rewards his good behavior along with keeping him in touch with his favorite teacher.

Our daily life is not easy, but we have found things that work for us. If I could offer advice to other parents, I would say, Be gentle with yourself. This is not a life that anyone plans on falling into, but there is never a dull moment. If you are married, you will probably have to make some adjustments within yourself and with your relationship in order for it to last. If you have other children, their lives will be affected by having a sibling with special needs. Sometimes it is for the good, and sometimes it is not. Find their interests, and don't forget that they need attention too. Reach out to others who have already experienced what you will go through. Most importantly, always trust your instincts.

Isaac has given us a new perspective and respect for human life in all its varied and unique manifestations. He has shown us how to be more compassionate and patient while challenging us along the way. Isaac shows us daily how smart he is. He has a unique ability to memorize places, people's names, floor plans, Google map locations, and numerous other things that typical folks could not comprehend. Our overall goal is to help Isaac use his smarts and unique abilities to achieve greatness in his own right. We have been exposed to a life we never knew existed. Although challenging at times, we would never change it.

This is a letter from one of his previous teachers:

> Tiffany, my exposure to you has been limited at best since my relationship with you has been through my adult-child relationship with Isaac. Employment position withstanding, I cannot deny I fell in love with Isaac from day one. He has the *hugest heart* of anyone I know—my husband and me not counting. You can tell him I said that because he has such a *huge* heart, so full of love, all the people who help him will love him too. They will make sure they do their best and work really hard to get him better and keep him better. On the last day of school, we had just sat down at the rug for circle time when Isaac looked at me and announced he had to go to the bathroom. I spontaneously got up to join him. As we left the room, he asked if he could hold my hand since he loves me. We are to discourage handholding since it is the preschool's job to prepare the children for kindergarten, and kindergarten teachers don't hold hands. My response came from my heart and feelings for Isaac: "Of course we can hold hands!"

> At the end of the day, the class was going towards the table for snack. There was noise with the transition, and Isaac, who was

bringing up the rear, turned and said to me as my hand was on the doorknob, "I love you!" Once again, I did what I am not supposed to do and, with a quick survey of who would hear me, I said "I love you" back, hoping that the teacher or the other children didn't hear me. As I walked down the hall, I cried because although I don't know Isaac's health issues, I realize his health is more than just fragile, and he was about to have a very serious procedure that could jeopardize his life. I also thought that if an adult did hear and reported me, I might get fired. I can think of worse things to lose a job over. Isaac brought joy to me every day, and loving your child meant more to me than protocol. Knowing Isaac has been a true blessing and gift, and having him in my life has been the best present ever!

I believe that life is not random, but that we meet and have people in our lives for a reason. In the case of Isaac and me, it could be simply for pure love to be shared with an incredibly special person.

Chapter 6

Young Adults

Part of the fear associated with a diagnosis of Williams syndrome is the uncertainty about the future, not knowing what to expect. And the best cure for that fear is getting to know young adults with Williams syndrome and seeing how they thrive and what they have accomplished. They are proof that while Williams syndrome is a facet of their lives; it does not have to define them.

My Son, the Non-Brain Surgeon
Maggie Covar

Maggie Covar has one child, Bryan, who has Williams syndrome. They currently reside in Tampa, Florida. They both enjoy spending time at the beach, listening to music, and spending time with friends.

Bryan was born in 1989 and diagnosed in 1991 with Williams syndrome when he was two-and-a-half years old. Williams syndrome was relatively unknown then. At that time, there was not any formal testing, no FISH test, and no microarray analysis. Diagnoses of Williams syndrome were made based mainly on facial and physical characteristics. I still remember the doctor examining my son and then walking out of the room without saying a word. He returned with a book that was opened to a page that had pictures of what I thought were abused children. He finally spoke and said, "Your son has Williams syndrome just like the children in those pictures." He then suggested that I put him in a state institution and let the state take care of him. His reasoning was that in a couple of years, Bryan would be so physically and mentally handicapped that even I, as his mother, would not want to look at or take care of him.

My mother was with me at this doctor's appointment, and her response was, "That is never going to happen. What else can we do to help him?" The doctor responded that we did not understand; he said that this child would never have the ability to be a brain surgeon, and my mother responded that she didn't either. The doctor said that we had no idea what Bryan would be capable of or his life expectancy. He went on, stating that raising this child would be hard work and that he was a child that most people would not want. My mother responded, "I have raised seven children, and when each one was born, I had no idea what life had in store for them. I had no idea what their capabilities were, nor their life expectancy. Each child was hard work, so tell me what makes this child any different?" We left that doctor's office and never returned.

A year later, we went to the Boston Children's Hospital and received the same diagnosis but with a much different approach. The message was the same—we had no idea about what the future holds—but the outlook was much brighter. The possibilities, they said, are endless. The doctors at the Boston clinic offered support. They suggested contacting the Williams Syndrome Association and also discussed options for my son.

Today, Bryan is twenty-four years old, and he is amazing. He has achieved many things in his life. Life has been a journey. Sure, he has his good days and bad days, difficulties and successes, just like anyone does in life. Bryan loves life, people, and music. Since Bryan was a year old, he has shown signs of incredible musical talent. Musical instruments are the focus in Bryan's bedroom. He has a love for harmonicas, drums, and the keyboard, and he has taught himself to play all of these instruments. He started to play the harmonica when he was about two years old. He cannot read music, but give him a drumstick or a harmonica and he can repeat a song. His dream is to start his own band one day. Bryan is a natural entertainer. He has no fear of being in front of a large audience, and he can get a crowd moving and dancing. He has performed on the Grand Ole Opry stage on five different occasions while attending the Lifting Lives Music Camp at the Vanderbilt Kennedy Center. For several years, he has been honored with playing the harmonica, and sometimes he has played a short harmonica solo. He has appeared on national television, performing with Darius Rucker and other individuals with Williams syndrome at the MGM Grand in Las Vegas, Nevada, on the Academy of Country Music Awards show.

Honestly, I have to say, Bryan probably would not have made a good brain surgeon, as he hates needles and blood. His passion is music, and he is good at it. Many musicians have a dream of performing on the Grand Ole Opry stage, but not many can say that they have achieved that dream. Bryan knows what he wants to do in life and is working toward his goal.

My mom told me that if all you do is focus on his disability, all you will do is focus on what he cannot do. Just imagine the possibilities if you focus on his capabilities. Recently, I asked Bryan to describe his disabilities to me. Shocked and with disbelief in his voice, he replied, "I'm disabled?" "Oh," I said. "Tell me about your abilities." Relieved, he quickly replied, "I am a musician. I am nice. I am friendly. I am funny. I am smart. I am a great person, and I am a great son. Oh, yeah, and I am amazing."

Over the past few years, I have come to realize that parents all want the same basic things for their children. They want them to be happy, to have all their needs met, and to be successful. I have asked several people to define *successful,* and each had a different definition. Basically, the common denominator is that their child gets to live his or her dream. Then, I realized that is it—the dream. By that definition, my son is successful. His dream is to be a musician, to have friends who love music, and to always have music in his life. A smile came to my face as I realized that my son is living his dream.

Who needs a brain surgeon? I have a very happy and talented son who is amazing. He is living his dream. What more could a mother want for her amazing son?

God Only Gives Us What We Can Handle
Tamey Harper

Tamey Harper is the mother of three children. She resides in Northeastern Oklahoma where she and Tedi are two happening chicks.

As a frightened, twenty-one-year-old single mother, I gave birth to a healthy baby girl on Monday, September 28, 1987. As she grew, I grew alongside her, loving and living as we both endured and enjoyed  each other daily. Soon, we met a man who wanted to share his life with us; we married, and I became pregnant with another child. Life seemed to be coming together in a wonderful way. One unusually warm January day, while playing outside, my sweet four-year-old baby girl started a conversation with Jesus that she couldn't finish here on Earth. The next three weeks were an emotional blur of hate, regret, fear, longing, and resentment. How could I be prepared for the next beautiful moment in my life when I was reeling from a very tragic experience? The arrival of a precious little boy just three weeks after the death of my only child was beyond comprehension. Only a mother who has lost a child can relate, and she wishes she couldn't. I mourned one child and welcomed another in less than a month. Joseph saved my life. Without him, I cannot say that I would have survived. People, meaning well, said to me, "God only gives us what we can handle."

Two years later, I learned that I was pregnant with a baby girl. Confusion set in about whether I was ready to face the possibility of another girl. Would I be ready to love and accept this child? Would I compare this little girl to the light of my life that was extinguished so quickly? The due date was predicted to be the same September day for our new little girl. I swallowed hard and pretended to be all right. My throat closed on the elevator ride to each doctor's appointment while I anticipated the worst in myself and in God; after all, He did believe I could handle the worst.

I scheduled her arrival for September 20, 1994. This would make it easier on everyone. No need to encourage the comparisons by sharing a birthday with her older sister. Tedi wasn't like either of the two children before her. She was small and frail and cried a lot. Her two-year-old brother, Joseph, thought we should exchange her for another because "this one cries too much." Even with the known diagnosis of Williams syndrome at one month old, it was hard to accept the road ahead. But I had faced much worse scenarios, and all I needed was a plan.

The assistance of another mother of a child with Williams syndrome helped us prepare for our future challenges. My early conversations with Pam enlightened me to the possibility of Tedi living a full life. Her daughter, Chelsea, was graduating from high school the year Tedi was born. Eighteen months of Tedi's relentless crying and my tears of exhaustion produced a beautiful, curious, loving child with the face of an angel. She didn't eat solid food until she was four years old. That was also when she began to speak in full sentences, seemingly overnight. Expert high-speed crawling was replaced with walking at five years of age. Milestone after delayed milestone was reached in its own time. Countless challenges in the form of surgeries and nights of lost sleep were to follow, but we endured, as mothers and daughters do. As Tedi says, "We're just a couple of happening chicks from Broken Arrow."

It has been our experiences together that have made us a family. The challenges we have faced through Tedi's medical and conditional situations have shaped us into a better group of human beings. The tolerance for other, seemingly different families wasn't quite as strong as it is now, knowing what others may be experiencing. Our exposure to physical and occupational therapists, other medical professionals, insurance professionals, and hospital surroundings has made us quite aware of which procedures can go smoothly and which may not. The emotional roller coaster of, "Am I making the right choices for her future?" followed with "Could I have done something differently to have avoided the surgeries?" is overwhelming at times.

My strength comes from Tedi. When I am spinning out in space with questions and concerns, she possesses the ability to bring me right back to Earth. During her third heart surgery—this was the one when they patched her heart with some of her own tissue to correct the aortic stenosis—the surgeon stopped her heart for forty-five minutes. She had been in a drug-induced sleep for four days. As a mother, I was concerned because she hadn't eaten. Her complexion was a gray color that I cannot describe. Still distraught, I had to return to work that fifth morning, with no vacation or sick time remaining. I left my mother in the room with Tedi. Following work, I returned to the hospital to find that Tedi was indeed awake and eating. She had been checked out of the ICU and moved to another floor. I quickly located the new room and walked in to find Tedi sitting on the edge of the bed eating ice cream. Her thirteen-year-old face lit up as she exclaimed, "Mom, you will not believe how sick these poor kids are in this hospital!" I said, "I know, and you are one of them." She thought for a minute and replied, "I am fine. They are really in trouble, and some of them need a visitor really bad." Tedi already wanted to set up a system of support for the "sick" children she had seen on the gurney ride from the ICU. The fact that her chest had been cut from sternum to navel had no effect on her perception of the other children's needs. The ability to see someone else's trouble above your own and the need to help are gifts that God gives children with Williams syndrome.

God had given me what I can handle. It came in the form of a beautiful baby girl who would bless me with her wisdom and her ability to love in any situation. He blessed me with a child who could find no fault in the world, a child who reminds me every day of what we should all be living for—each other. Years before, I had inscribed her sister's monument with a personal note; it reads, "On the day you were born, I thanked God for letting me know you. Your openness to love inspires me to open my heart as I have never done before." I thought that feeling was buried with that child, but it was renewed in my sense of good and God with Tedi.

Tedi Marie Harper is eighteen years old and graduated from Broken Arrow High School in May 2013. She is full of love and grace for everyone she meets. Her ability to welcome anyone into her inner circle, no matter what the challenge, is inspiring to all who meet her. Tedi wants to work with animals. She is interested in a job that will meet her need to share a love of animals with the people who love them. Her love of the automatic car wash seems to soothe her when she is stressed, and she shares her experiences in a personal blog. We are currently working on making her blog public so she can share her compiled knowledge with the world. Look for Tedi's Car Wash Extravaganza blog in the near future. It is sure to be as entertaining, inspiring, and enlightening as Tedi herself.

That Something Special

Terry Monkaba

Terry Monkaba lives in Michigan with her husband, Gary. They have two sons, Ben and Adam. Terry loves traveling, photography, videography, and most of all, helping others along their journey with Williams syndrome.

It's hard to believe now, but twenty-six years ago, when I was pregnant with Ben, having your first child at thirty-five was considered "old." But we were thrilled, and my husband, Gary, and I approached this special time with all the attention we had given our careers. We made recordings of each other reading our favorite children's books and played both those and Vivaldi's *Four Seasons* to our unborn son each evening. We practiced breathing in Lamaze classes so we would be ready for natural childbirth. Then, after a very benign pregnancy, my labor and delivery started us out on a journey much different from the one we had envisioned.

After several hours of labor and no dilation, the doctor broke my water to try and speed along the process. A short time later, he determined that our baby was in distress, and since I was nowhere near ready to deliver him naturally, a C-section was performed. Doctors then found that the baby had aspirated meconium, and he was rushed off to a neighboring hospital where there was a neonatal intensive care unit. It would be five long days before I was released from the hospital and could visit my son. When Ben was placed in my arms for the first time, I couldn't stop crying. We were finally a family, and Ben was given a clean bill of health. His only remaining hurdle seemed to be learning to suck and swallow.

The next five weeks flew by, with Gary and me adjusting to parenthood, Ben learning to eat, and the house bustling with visitors. We were amazed that Ben actually seemed to recognize the recordings that I had dutifully played for him during the pregnancy, and they clearly had a calming effect whenever he was upset. Everything was great!

And then, one morning, Ben didn't seem like himself to me. I called his doctor and was told I could bring Ben in later that morning. The doctor found an inguinal hernia that was probably the source of his discomfort, but she also heard a heart murmur for the first time and told me we would need to learn more about that before getting the hernia fixed. I remember that she very calmly told me that I should probably drive straight to the hospital. She would call ahead to tell them we were coming, and she would call my husband and have him meet us there. It would be three months before we got home again, and nearly five months would pass before we finally got that hernia repaired. When we did, it wasn't Ben's first surgery—it was his fourth. The three cardiovascular repairs that came first not only put our son's survival in question; they came in tandem with the diagnosis of Williams syndrome and a brand new course to all of our lives, a course that we could never have imagined.

There are many characteristics that are common to Williams syndrome, but the one that defines our son is a unique spirit and positive outlook that often manifests itself in pure joy. It is a spirit that has not only helped Ben overcome many obstacles; it has also had an impact on so many others who have come in contact with him throughout his twenty-six years. Ben is truly an optimist, a young man who simply chooses to find beauty and joy not just in special occasions, but in everyday activities as well. More importantly, he never keeps his feelings to himself. He readily shares them with everyone he meets.

Ben was talking before he was two, and his first words—"Hi, how're you?"—were uttered to everyone we met with a big, beautiful smile. He was afraid of the dentist, and early appointments were difficult. But no matter how much he cried throughout the appointment, each visit ended with him wiping the tears from his eyes and exclaiming, "Thank you, dental officers. I know you took good care of me." He often had the nurses in tears as we left. Parent-teacher and IEP meetings included statements of wonder at the fact that Ben always noted when a hairstyle was changed, nails had been painted a new color, or a new outfit was worn, and he always told the teachers how beautiful the changes were.

If Ben didn't like a particular teacher or therapist, he would never tell us they were mean or bad teachers. I would ask, "How do you like Mrs. Jones, Ben?" and he would respond, "She is doing her best, Mom." While in high school, Ben insisted on attending the homecoming dance alone. When I picked him up at the end of the evening, he was briefly despondent because all the girls had dates, and not many of them had agreed to dance with him. However, it took him only a short time to review the evening again and decide that he was glad he went after all because the girls looked beautiful in their dresses and had told him they liked his new suit.

Ben invited popular girls to every school dance or special event but did so without ever putting them in an awkward situation. His invitation always started with, "You are probably too busy but ..." or "I bet someone already asked you but ..." Consequently, the girls always used whatever excuse he provided, but they were also very kind to him, and he ended every conversation with, "Well, okay, maybe next time then," and he felt very good about himself for trying.

Ben is now twenty-six and proud to be a young adult. But he's not too proud to enjoy the spirit of the holidays and the simple joys of life. We visited a Christmas village today that included a laser light show. As the lights went down, the audience was encouraged to sing along with the holiday favorites, and one audience member did just that. Ben sang every song, oohed and aahed at every laser, and clapped the loudest at the end of the show. There was also a wonderful Santa, and Ben couldn't stay away, exclaiming that he wouldn't sit on his lap because he was an adult now, but he would love to say hi because "I'm a kid at heart, Mom, and it's part of the Christmas tradition." Ben walked up to Santa with his hand outstretched, and Santa stood up to shake hands with him, exclaiming that it was nice to see Ben again. (Great Santa!) They spoke for a few seconds, and then Santa asked Ben what he wanted for Christmas. Ben's reply was, "I'm an adult now, Santa, and I don't need gifts, but my friend Kristin has been very good, and I hope you will get her something nice."

There are times when, like every parent of a child with special challenges, I wish that Ben were doing better. But I have only to spend an afternoon like the one we shared today to remember that we all have challenges, regardless of whether or not they come with a label. And despite the challenges, Ben has much to offer and so often reminds me of what is important in this life and of what we should truly cherish. Ben is quite simply … something special.

Chapter 7

International Perspectives

Williams syndrome knows no bounds—it pays no attention to a person's ethnicity, sex, or country of origin. Likewise, the Williams syndrome community also knows no bounds. People with Williams syndrome live in countries across the globe, and we are lucky to hear four of their stories.

That Fighting Spirit
Jeanine Coetzee

Jeanine Coetzee, now Mrs. Burger, is Johan Coetzee's older sister. She and her husband, Corné, live in Keetmanshoop, Namibia, where Jeanine holds a primary school teaching post in music. She also teaches Afrikaans, English, and mathematics.

Johan Coetzee, born on November 1, 1993, has been a true inspiration to our family and to many across South Africa with his unfailing fighting spirit!

Small at birth and developmentally delayed, he reached all of his milestones at a later stage, taking his first steps at thirty-two months and making Mom run excitedly through the house yelling, "Johan can walk! Come see! Johan can walk!" His first words—"ta ta," which means "bye-bye" or "let's go visiting"—came only after the age of four.

We have witnessed Johan's special sprit in every aspect of his life, from medical and educational challenges to finding ways to enrich his life with music, to making a difference in his community by reaching out to *all,* and finally to accepting people for who they are regardless of status. Throughout his life, he has had to undergo a series of very

scary surgeries, and each time his miraculous progress has made an impact on the medical staff who treated him and his family. The first surgery took place when he was just one month old, and stenosis had completely shut down his pyloric valve. In 2003, when he was just nine years old, his life was yet again saved by emergency surgery—this time a double heart bypass. The most miraculous recovery, however, was in 2011 when his colon ruptured, and doctors thought there was no hope of saving him. Family and friends around the world went on their knees together to pray for a miracle, and once again this courageous young man defied all odds and made a full recovery.

And he shares his special spirit with others. Even when he is in an amazing amount of pain, Johan reaches out, making friends with the other ICU patients, staff, and visitors. He helps by encouraging them through their own difficult times and by raising awareness for his genetic difference, handing out pamphlets to doctors, staff, and patients. In a world where most of us guard our emotions and remain carefully detached, Johan makes a difference, touching lives with his unique personality and a maturity found in very few people his age.

Johan's hopes for learning how to read and write were crushed after just two weeks in first grade, when his teacher recommended that he be removed from formal schooling as it was clear that he would not be able to keep up. Yet again, his fighting spirit rose to the challenge and, with the help of his devoted mother, he learned at home. Johan took his education upon himself by visiting the library a few blocks from home, where he was well known and much loved. Taking the librarian by the hand, he asked her to help him search for books on his current favorite topic (often in the nonfiction, adult book section). Johan's learning started with books on trains for weeks and weeks and then moved on to trucks, and on and on. This was followed by fire engines, tankers, battleships, submarines, and more. These informative books were mostly in English, which Mom had to read day after day with Johan sitting on her lap, taking it all in. In this way, he soon became able to read, write, and calculate basic math problems.

With the ability to read and write, Johan has taught himself skills in many other areas. An avid drummer, he uses the Internet to learn new beats and techniques. He received his first drum set from Reach for a Dream after undergoing the emergency double heart bypass in 2003. With the help of a music therapist, he started slowly but soon became increasingly proficient and has since moved on to other instruments as well. When he turned twelve, he received a guitar and dreamed about becoming a rock star like the popular South African singer/guitarist Steve Hofmeyr and singing on stage with him at a concert held that year. Once again, he started slowly, picking the instrument up on occasion and playing *with* it. But when he had just turned sixteen years of age, and the time was right for him, he suddenly started playing his guitar as a true musician—picking out any song that came to mind and playing each note correctly. Johan does not just play music; he lives the music. And that special relationship with music is so evident to all who listen that they find him truly inspirational.

Johan is fluent in English with a nearly flawless accent. His desire to learn and his fighting spirit were all he needed. Through the Internet and television, Johan taught himself and has recently started to learn German as he watches online videos about fire rescue operations around Germany.

Johan has many interests, but none is greater than his love for emergency services. And, true to form, Johan has found ways to learn more than most of us could ever dream when it comes to police, fire, road, and sea safety. Throughout his life, John has been a frequent visitor at the East London Flying Squad (Police), the fire station, and the National Sea Rescue Institute Stations near his home. At each visit, Johan spreads his special spirit and his love for all the men and women who are keeping his community safe. The special friends he has made there will go to great lengths to make every visit amazingly memorable, and they often go well "beyond the call of duty" for Johan—even making special trips to visit him and arranging for Johan and his parents to experience the thrill of riding on emergency equipment, not just on land and sea but even in a helicopter.

Through Facebook searches, Johan has introduced himself, in a very "Johan sort of way," to famous South African television presenter and executive producer Johan Stemmet from the program *Noot vir Noot* (*Note for Note*), the longest continually running television game show on South African television. Mr. Stemmet has subsequently invited Johan to the recording of Program Number 40 at the South African Broadcasting Company's studio, where he will have the opportunity to join the well-known Musiek Fabriek Band and perform a song of his choice in front of a live audience.

Johan's life is full because he has made it so. Our family has helped along the way, but much of what Johan has accomplished, both socially and with the skills he has gained, has been due to his personal fighting spirit. Through his spirit, his drive, and his love for mankind, Johan makes a difference in his world every day.

My Katy

Merry Burrows

After more than thirty years working in the IT industry for multinational companies in both the UK and the USA, Merry took an early retirement and, among other things, is now the treasurer and a trustee of the UK Williams Syndrome Foundation. She has been a member of the foundation for more than twenty years.

Merry lives with her dog, Liquorice, in Portsmouth in the UK close to her two children, Matthew, who is twenty-eight, and Katy, who is twenty-seven and has Williams syndrome.

December 1986 to September 1987

I had a normal pregnancy with Katy, my second child, but I was completely unprepared for the impact that her birth would have on my life.

Katy was born on Christmas Eve in 1986. My first memory of her birth is being told, "It's a girl," and then, "She has a cleft palate." They sent for the pediatrician and, within five minutes, the cleft palate diagnosis was dismissed. She was declared to have a heart condition and was quickly taken to the Special Care Baby Unit.

We stayed in the hospital for three weeks, first in Special Care, where Katy was unfairly known as "Big Fat Kate" because at six pounds,

thirteen ounces, she was huge compared to the premature babies. Then we moved to the infectious diseases ward because she contracted bronchiolitis and had to be isolated from the tiny babies. There, we lived in a glass cage, looking at other families in adjacent glass cages. Katy was very sick, and I had to weigh her before and after every meal. She would not be allowed home until she gained weight.

Always a survivor, Katy recovered from the bronchiolitis and jaundice, and we were sent to the Cardiac Unit at Southampton Hospital, where the doctors investigated her heart condition. Eventually, Katy was diagnosed with a hole in her heart and was allowed to go home. She would need regular check-ups and probably an operation when she was about three.

Then began eight months of sleepless nights. Katy never slept for more than two consecutive hours. She was obviously in discomfort, particularly when lying down. Most of the day, we hung her from the doorframe in a baby bouncer as this was the only position in which she was content. I read the warnings that said, "Do not leave your child in this bouncer for more than thirty minutes" with despair. At night, I used an old-fashioned pram and pushed her up and down as this seemed to soothe her.

When she was nine months old, we went to the hospital for a check-up. After X-rays and an echocardiogram, the doctors decided she needed angioplasty. They found valvular problems and decided to operate. Apparently, her condition was so serious that her heart could have stopped beating at any time.

The tests continued the next day, and the surgeon said that he was reasonably certain that Katy had Williams syndrome. He said that she would be mentally challenged (but used a more derogatory term), "small in stature and unlikely to live long depending on the success or failure of her heart surgery." He gave me a photocopy from a medical journal, and months later I managed to translate it with the help of a dictionary. My husband, Mark, handled the diagnosis very well, telling me that it would be okay. He said that Katy would probably end up as a chat show host or a politician.

We were taken for a tour of the children's intensive care unit so we could see someone else's child on a ventilator and not be too shocked when we saw our own child there. The next morning I bathed Katy in some pink antiseptic lotion before her pre-med injection. This didn't impress her at all, and she yelled loudly. We took her to the operating room, where the nurses had obviously been told to keep the baby with her parents for as long as possible. However, laying Katy into a cot full of ice and covering her with an ice blanket before watching her get an anesthetic injection is something that I still have nightmares about today. I kissed Katy good-bye, and we were told to come back in six hours. We had coffee and went shopping, buying a teddy bear that still sleeps on Katy's bed. Eventually, it was time for us to return to the hospital, where we were told that the operation had gone well.

I knew what to expect, but I was still shocked upon seeing my tiny little baby in a large white bed with a breathing machine covering her whole face. They had taken my baby away and made eleven entry and exit holes in her body. The worst was a drain hole below her breastbone, which can still be clearly seen today. She was naked apart from a few plasters, and her skin was stained yellow with iodine. Her breathing was labored and loud, which I supposed was from the machine. I touched her gently and was relieved that she was at least warm.

I spent the evening and all night alternating between sitting in the ICU waiting for Katy to wake up and trying to sleep in my room at the hospital. I remember writing a long letter to a friend and, to my shame, thinking that it would be better if Katy didn't survive if she was to be severely mentally challenged and sickly. But with the benefit of hindsight, I was definitely so wrong!

The next morning, I found Katy awake and doing so well that the doctors planned to remove the breathing machine. If she managed well, she would be in the children's cardiac ward in time for lunch. I had been told to expect her to be in intensive care for at least forty-eight hours! I held her hand as they switched off the breathing machine. It must have been quite an effort because she fell asleep again, but this time with no labored breathing from the machine. Later that morning, she was taken to the ward. When I got there, she was sitting up in her cot and smiling! Katy didn't smile often, and to see it was nothing short of miraculous. My picky daughter, who never ate more than the smallest mouthful of anything, was ravenously hungry. I fed her two scoops of mashed potatoes, spaghetti hoops, and a beefburger—not the healthiest of meals but the first that she ever appeared to have enjoyed. For the next eighteen years, I don't think she stopped eating or asking for food!

Katy recovered extremely quickly and stayed in the hospital for only one week. Back home, she gave up the baby bouncer and switched her attention to the baby walker. She would whizz round and round the kitchen floor, giving much pleasure to all who saw her.

Katy was mostly an absolute joy during her childhood and has grown up to be a sympathetic, polite, kind, generous, and entertaining young lady, albeit one who agonizes far too deeply over her own and other people's misfortunes. She also has a propensity to get herself into difficult situations and loves the drama. Today, Katy lives independently in her own flat and works happily as a volunteer for a local theater. I do still see her every day and help her to manage some aspects of her life, but she has done so well and achieved so much that I am immensely proud of her!

In her own words: "I know that I will have Williams for the rest of my life, but I can be strong and I can do anything if I try hard enough."

A Letter to My Son

Blaise Dobbin

Blaise Dobbin and his wife, Michelle, have a fifteen-year-old daughter, Megan, and a twelve-year-old son, Nolan, who has Williams syndrome. They live in Sackville, New Brunswick, Canada, and are currently the provincial chapter contacts for the Canadian Association for Williams Syndrome.

Last summer we attended the Williams Syndrome Association conference in Boston, and one of the workshops I attended while there was the Parent's Heart Inspirational Writing Seminar facilitated by Ani Tuzman. As part of that session, we were given five minutes to write a letter to our child with Williams syndrome. The following is my letter word-for-word as composed in those five minutes:

Dear Nolan,

When I learned that you had Williams syndrome, I was sad. I was sad because of the medical issues. I was sad because of the challenges and struggles you would certainly face in this world. I was sad because this wasn't what Mommy and I had expected or wanted for you. I guess it seemed like our dreams of "what you would be" had been ripped away from us.

As you grow, I grow too. I am growing to understand that you are a true blessing in our lives. I see it in how you have brought Mommy and Daddy closer together in a true spiritual way. I see it in how you have taught your sister, Megan, to be patient, accepting, gracious, and interested in people of diversity. Most of all, I see how you continue to touch and teach those around you in your community and in every situation you find yourself.

Thank you for your gifts. I love you. I am so blessed.

Daddy

I've compiled a collection of funny or amusing stories and experiences with Nolan, which I'd like to share with you.

February 9, 2013 (Age 11)

While watching TV: "The following program contains coarse language that some viewers may find offensive." Nolan replied, "Don't worry. I won't be offended."

February 6, 2013 (Age 11)

Nolan's rebuttal to me upon hearing me complain about Louie (our dog): "I love Louie just the way he is. I love the way he plays. I love the way he jumps. I love the way he runs. I love the way he kicks up the grass after he craps. What's not to love?"

December 23, 2012 (Age 11)

After weeks of preparing for the Christmas Eve mass youth choir (with Megan in the bells section and Nolan in the voice section), Nolan approached the choir director this morning at the end of the last practice and told her, "I'm not singing tomorrow night. I'm too old for this choir, and I think this is stupid. Fa-la-la-la-la-la-la-la-la!"

December 19, 2012 (Age 11)

We have always packed a $10.00 "emergency fund" in the kids' school bags for "emergencies" like missing lunches or unexpected book fairs. I believe Megan still has the same $10.00 from her kindergarten emergency fund. Nolan's fund, however, is more of an emergency "budget." Even as a seasoned sales professional, I can't for the life of me imagine how I could possibly pitch a $7.00 bag of Twizzlers licorice as an "emergency."

December 16, 2012 (Age 11)

Following bedtime prayers, Nolan shouts across the hall, "Megan, when you go to heaven, can I have your iPod touch?" Needless to say, his sister will be sleeping with one eye open.

November 26, 2012 (Age 11)

While Nolan and I were out for another chilly walk tonight, he told me that he feels the same way about walking as he does about going to church. I told him that as long as he lived with me, he would need to get exercise. He scoffed at that notion, saying, "Well, if you and Mom ever split and get divorced, I'm moving in with her so I can lie on the couch and watch TV all day." So I asked, "What if Mom gets a new boyfriend?" Nolan replied, "Well, I hope he likes TV!"

November 25, 2012 (Age 11)

Nolan is not a big fan of walking (understatement), so when I dragged him out for a long cold walk this afternoon, I told him to "look up the word *fun* in the dictionary and you will see 'A long walk with dad,'" to which he immediately growled, "Yeah, then look up the word *bumface*, and you will see a picture of YOU!"

October 17, 2012 (Age 11)

Nolanism of the day: While peeing almost exclusively on the upright toilet seat cover this morning, Nolan glances back over his shoulder and says, "You know, Dad, it's really too bad we don't have a urinal in here," to which I replied, "Yeah, I hear ya, son."

October 2, 2012 (Age 11)

Nolan: "I don't know who I want to go out with at Halloween this year."
Megan: "What about me, Nolan? I would like to go with you at Halloween this year."
Nolan (with a rather indignant tone): "Like I just said, Megan, I don't know who I would like to go out with this year!"

August 25, 2012 (Age 10)

Me: "So, Megan, what do you think you will be doing ten years from now?"

Megan: "Um, let's see … I'll be working on my second university degree or perhaps already starting my career."

Me: "Nolan, how about you?"

Nolan: "Ten years from now, I will be living in a big mansion, pool in the backyard, Lamborghini, supermodel for a wife, and *no kids*!"

Easter Nolan story

So we walk to church only to meet the caretaker in the driveway, who tells us mass is cancelled. From the corner of my eye I see a fist pump and a silent but clearly mouthed "Yes!" from Nolan. As we turn to walk home, Nolan takes my hand and says, "Dad, I'm so disappointed church is cancelled, especially since it is Easter and I have my snazzy clothes on. This is total bull crap!" When we get home, I say, "Well, we can say some prayers together," to which Nolan replies, "Naw, I'm good."

March 23, 2012 (Age 10)

Nolan: "That sucks!"

Me: "How about saying something like, 'That's unfortunate'?"

Nolan: "Naw, I like 'sucks' better. Thanks, though."

Nolan: "Dad, how do I win money at this swim meet?"

Me: "Well, you have to swim all three events, including the 50-meter backstroke."

Nolan: "The 50-meter backstroke? Frig that, Dad. I have tons of money at home."

January 20, 2012 (Age 10)

Nolanism of the week: "Dad, there are two things I like in a movie … awesomeness and violence!"

October 10, 2011 (Age 10)

The kids were very excited when we told them that instead of going to church on Sunday morning, we were going to go on a family outing at Ski Wentworth, where they had the chair lift running for their Festival of Colour (ride up and hike back down). When we got on the chair lift,

Nolan was terrified and exclaimed, "We're all going to die! Oh, God, I wish we went to church instead!"

March 28, 2011 (Age 9)

Leader of the local Scouting Movement: "Nolan, so are you in Beavers or Cubs this year?"
Nolan: "Neither … I'm too old for that. Those kids are nothin' but a bunch of nerds."

May 5, 2010 (Age 8)

Nolan told us randomly at supper last night that he wants "to get the new Equinox." When I asked why, he replied (not without a certain amount of indignation), "Dad, it's the most fuel efficient crossover on the highway." Do you think he watches too much TV?

Our Princess Dianne

Janice Rowley

Janice Rowley has two girls, Dianne and Sharon. They live in Victoria, Australia. Dianne is on Facebook and loves speaking to people with Williams syndrome over the computer.

Dianne was fifteen years old before we found out that she has Williams syndrome. At the time, people asked what would happen if she did not have Williams syndrome, and we said nothing because, to us, Dianne is Dianne. We did not need a name for what was wrong, but it was nice to have one.

Dianne had to be taught everything, having both speech and occupational therapy for nine years from the age of three. Our friends always called her a pixie when she was a little girl because she was so small. Our friends used to put her in a pram and have her as their doll,

which was funny when people did not know and the doll moved. Dianne did not walk until she was two years and six months old, which was not an issue because of her size. People thought that she was a lot younger.

Dianne went to a typical school until the age of ten and then transferred to a special school until she turned eighteen. She then worked as a volunteer for eighteen years at the school she attended originally. She assisted the children with reading and art. Dianne is now going to a special adult center, which she loves. Among the programs offered, Dianne asked if she could go on the radio (to myself, I was thinking she had to be joking), but after two years she now has her own program. She presents a half-hour music program every week on the local radio channel. People can pick it up on the computer at 104.7 FM Gippsland on Saturday night at 5:30 p.m. Australia time. We are so proud of her, and every week she just gets better.

Dianne has always been a challenge because Williams syndrome was not well known in Australia before she was diagnosed. There was no help or advice available at that time, not that it would have changed the way that we needed to work with her. Today, Dianne leads a very busy life as she is on the go six days of the week. She has day placements five days and does Ten Pin Bowling forty-four Saturdays of the year. She has been involved with this for twenty-four years.

She still lives with us and always will. Dianne has achieved well over her thirty-nine years, but she will never be able to live independently. She is unable to cook and has a go at the washing but is not so good at cleaning. I do not know what other Williams syndrome adults are like, so it will be interesting to find out at the conference how the older people with Williams syndrome are coping with life.

Dianne's main wish at the moment is to go the conference next year. She has been twice before—once in Salt Lake City and also in San Diego. She has her fortieth birthday this year so, instead of presents, we are going to suggest donations for the airfare, which will help with the costs. We hope to meet new friends there.

Part III

Reflections from Adults with Williams Syndrome

Terry Monkaba, Executive Director of the Williams Syndrome Association, asked nine adults with Williams syndrome the following two questions:
  1) What did your parent(s) do for you that helped the most?
  2) What advice do you have for younger people with Williams syndrome that might help them?
Their answers, presented in the following section, are a great resource for parents who are still raising their children and wondering what they could do better.

Tori Ackley (30 years old)—*Tori lives with other young adults and a care provider in South Hadley, Massachusetts. A graduate of the Berkshire Hills Music Academy (BHMA), she is an accomplished pianist and vocalist. Tori is a member of BHMA's performance troupe and the KANDOO Band. The two groups, which perform throughout Western Massachusetts, are composed entirely of young adults with Williams syndrome and other special challenges. Tori's other interests are writing music, spending time with her boyfriend, and enjoying community activities with her friends.*

1) What did your parent(s) do for you that helped the most?
   "My parents were always there for me. They stood by me in tough times. I got teased a lot in school and didn't have many friends, but my parents helped me get through it."

2) What advice do you have for younger people with Williams syndrome that might help them?
   "My music is what keeps me strong. When something is bothering me, I sit down and write a song about it. I love living on my own. I'm happy with myself, and that's important."

John Libera (31 years old)—*John lives in Massachusetts. He has his own apartment, which he shares with a young man without a disability who offers both companionship and security. He receives assistance with his shopping, cooking, and cleaning from a residential aide, who helps him for a few hours a day for up to five days a week. John works as a musician with the support of the vocational program in music at BHMA, where he is a longtime member of the Performance Troupe. He also performs with the KANDOO Band and with his church choir. His other interests are watching his favorite sports teams on television, reading the daily newspaper, and traveling. In the summer, he works as an assistant teacher at a recreational program for children with special needs, which*

recognized him with an award as "an ideal model of self-advocacy and independence."

1) What did your parent(s) do for you that helped the most?
   "Parents should encourage their kids to always try new things. That's what my mom and dad did."

2) What advice do you have for younger people with Williams syndrome that might help them?
   "My music is what I love, and I love my musician friends too. If you love music, you should take lessons."

Amy Koch (47 years old)—*Amy lives with other adults with special challenges in a home managed by the Marbridge Foundation in Texas. Amy works twenty-plus hours per week as a supply specialist at a nearby hospital. She loves to play the piano and sing and especially enjoys visiting her friends with Williams syndrome at special events around the country.*

1) What did your parent(s) do for you that helped the most?

   "My parents were so frustrated when I was growing up because no one knew what was wrong with me. Finally, when the computers came along, I Googled 'happy people' and some of my other traits and found information on Williams syndrome. I showed it to my parents and said this might be what I have. So we had the FISH test done, and sure enough that was me. My parents have tried to help me every way they could, and it was very helpful to finally know what the problem was."

2) What advice do you have for younger people with Williams syndrome that might help them?
   "I would tell young people with Williams to never give up on your dreams, no matter what anyone else tells you. Also, don't keep your feelings inside. When something is bothering you, it's important to tell someone and get it talked over, then move forward."

Kelley Martin (37 years old)—*Kelley lives in her own apartment in New Jersey. She is a graduate of Maplebrook School's CAP program and the BHMA, and she works as a hostess at a local Applebee's Restaurant. Kelley enjoys bowling and watching Broadway shows on television. She is also an ambassador for Special Olympics and competes in state and national games in track and field events and skiing. She looks forward to every Dream Team event so she can visit with her friends who have WS.*

1) What did your parent(s) do for you that helped the most?
"When I was little, I was terrified of thunderstorms and fireworks. I am trying really hard to get over the problem with fireworks. Thunderstorms—I wish we didn't have to have them. My parents helped me a lot and told me it was 'the angels bowling.'"

2) What advice do you have for younger people with Williams syndrome that might help them?
"I would tell young people to keep their heads up and do your best in school. Talk to a mentor about your problems. Come to the conventions; you make many friends and learn a lot."

Brett Glaser (27 years old)—*Brett lives with his parents in Madison, Connecticut. He helps provide security for the town of Madison and is also an elder care companion. He has a driver's license and enjoys reading, listening to music, watching football, playing poker, and hanging out with his friends when he is not working.*

1) What did your parent(s) do for you that helped the most?
"My mom sat with me every night until the homework was done and I did it correctly. She said, 'No giving up.' My parents told me that just because I have a disability, it is not an excuse. You still have to do your best. That was good advice for me."

2) What advice do you have for younger people with Williams syndrome that might help them?

"People told me 500 times, 'You'll never get your license to drive,' but I did it. So never give up on your goals, no matter what people tell you. You can do it if you put your mind to it."

Amy Berg (41 years old)—*Amy lives with her family in New Jersey. She celebrates her twentieth anniversary working for ACME supermarkets in 2014. Amy likes traveling and camping, visiting the casino, dinners out on the town, attending cultural festivals, and connecting with her friends via Facebook and WSA events.*

1) What did your parent(s) do for you that helped the most?
"My parents help me a lot with my money. They helped me with the issues I had with my disabled sister, and they helped with social and medical issues too."

2) What advice do you have for younger people with Williams syndrome that might help them?
"I would like to tell the younger kids who have WS to just follow your dreams, behave and have fun. Also, don't talk to strangers; if you need help, ask for it from someone you know. And above all, play music, dance, sing, and be joyful."

Avi Lesser (25 years old)—*Avi lives in a flat, independently with a roommate (also with special needs) in Illinois. Avi is so proud that he is living independently and is able to do this with the support of his family and an organization called Center for Independent Futures. Avi's primary job is as a pharmacy technician's assistant at Pharmore Drugs. He also works as cashier/barrista at The Perk, a not-for-profit coffee shop, which hires and trains adults with disabilities. Avi participates in several local social and recreational community-based programs for adults with intellectual disabilities and has attended the Williams Syndrome Music Camps for more than ten years! He loves music, piano, percussion, singing, and performing. He most recently* *performed as the opening act for The Temptations at a fund-raiser for more than 1,000 people. He rocked the house! Avi takes singing lessons and enjoys performing jug band music as much as opera. Avi's other interests are cooking, practicing other languages, and most especially learning other countries' national anthems. Avi has embraced a new philosophy for 2014 and beyond—Be Healthy: Eat Less and Move More!*

1) What did your parent(s) do for you that helped the most?
"My parents prepared me for moving out! They taught me to be independent so I could one day live on my own. Now I have my own room in a house with other guys, and it's great."

2) What advice do you have for younger people with Williams syndrome that might help them?
"I would tell a young person with Williams that it just doesn't matter. Everything is going to be all right. I am content."

Andrew Hamilton (37 years old)—*Andrew lives in Massachusetts in a managed home with other residents who have special challenges. He takes public transportation to his job at the library where he is in charge of shelving the "700s." Andrew participates in Special Olympics, goes to a weekly dance class, visits with his Best Bud, and likes browsing in video and comic book stores.*
He loves listening to music and speaks regularly about Williams syndrome, and living with a disability, to groups in the Boston area.

1) What did your parent(s) do for you that helped the most?
"My parents taught me to respect myself and other people. They taught me to be patient while learning something."

2) What advice do you have for younger people with Williams syndrome that might help them?

"I would tell a younger person with Williams that you should take not one day for granted. If you have problems, you need to talk them out. I work at a library and live in a group home. I have a very good support system around me. Life is good."

Marnie Meister (30 years old)—*Marnie lives in a home with several other residents with developmental disabilities in Wisconsin. She works at Endeavors Adult Development Center in Balsam Lake. Marnie can play piano, jump rope, sing and dance. And she loves to make people laugh.*

1) What did your parent(s) do for you that helped the most?

"My parents were always very supportive and loving. They were always there for me in the tough times. People with disabilities have many challenges, and sometimes people without disabilities don't realize that."

2) What advice do you have for younger people with Williams syndrome that might help them?

"I would say to a young person with Williams that we are so lucky to be cheerful and happy in our personalities. You can use that cheerfulness to help others who are feeling sad or lonely. I have a very happy and blessed life."

Thank you for taking the time to read our stories. For more information about Williams syndrome, please contact the Williams Syndrome Association (WSA). The WSA is the most comprehensive resource for people affected by Williams syndrome, as well as doctors, researchers, and educators.

williams-syndrome.org

Made in United States
Troutdale, OR
03/02/2024

18134875R00110